HUNTING HITLER

SOMDEV CHATTOPADHYAY

Copyright © Somdev Chattopadhyay
All Rights Reserved.

This book has been published with all efforts taken to make the material error-free after the consent of the author. However, the author and the publisher do not assume and hereby disclaim any liability to any party for any loss, damage, or disruption caused by errors or omissions, whether such errors or omissions result from negligence, accident, or any other cause.

While every effort has been made to avoid any mistake or omission, this publication is being sold on the condition and understanding that neither the author nor the publishers or printers would be liable in any manner to any person by reason of any mistake or omission in this publication or for any action taken or omitted to be taken or advice rendered or accepted on the basis of this work. For any defect in printing or binding the publishers will be liable only to replace the defective copy by another copy of this work then available.

This book is dedicated to Charanik

Contents

Foreword	*vii*
Preface	*ix*
Acknowledgements	*xiii*
Prologue	*xix*
1. Looking At Adolf Hitler's Last Days	1
2. Adolf Hitler's Last Witness	12
3. Adolf Hitler's Last Days	15
4. Life In The Führerbunker	21
5. Delight, Dismay And Disbelief	26
6. Mi5: The Hunt For Adolf Hitler	30
7. Fbi: Hitler's Death In The Führerbunker Is Questionable	34
8. Hitler In Argentina?	38
9. Hitler's Secret Argentine Sanctuary?	43
10. The Cia: He's Alive	51
11. Hitler In Colombia?	56
12. Cia Veteran Claims: Hitler 'faked His Own Death	62
13. The Real Story Of Hitler's Death?	66
14. 'hitler Lived'	74
15. Soviet Fake News	77
16. The Trevor-roper Dossier	80
17. The Flip Side Of Seeking Truth: 'overwhelming And Comprehensive' Evidence	82
18. The Skul, Jaws And Teeth	85
19. The Nazis Who Did Escape	90
20. America, A Haven For Hitler's Men	92
21. Adolf Hitler's Secret Agent In Cia	96

Contents

22. Mockups Of Hitler	99
23. Hitler Fled With Us Help	101
24. The Cia's Worst Kept Secret?	103
25. The National Police Gazette: Hitler In Antarctica	109
26. The Case Of Heinrich Himmler	114
27. The Nazi Expedition To Tibet	119
28. Savitri Devi: The Priestess Of Nazi	122
29. Life After Death?	124
30. Nanga Parvata: German Mountain Of Destiny In Kashmir Region	133
31. Kashmir: The Aryan Valley	136
32. Kashmir's Forgotten Chapter	139
33. Escape Submarine	146
34. Hitler: 'second Coming Of Jesus Christ'	149
35. Did Christ Escape To Kashmir?	151
36. Führer's Connection With The Maharajas	155
37. Could Hitler Be Buried In Kashmir?	161
38. Declassified Fbi Document	169
Epilogue	229

Foreword

This research-based book makes an attempt to find out the hidden threads of conspiracy theories regarding the death of Adolf Hitler and some of the deadly secrets. There are multiple layers, missing links and unfathomable legends that make the book thrilling and thoroughly enjoyable. It connects to the mystery of Netaji Subhas Chandra Bose's disappearance as well. Rare documents and images from international archives and other authentic sources make the book a precious one.

Preface

Smetacek was a Sudeten German Czech who fled from the Nazis in Calcutta in 1939. He is said to have been involved in a plot to dynamite a railway tunnel in the Sudetenland but was discovered by the Gestapo. The plot was against Hitler when he visited the Sudetenland in the spring of 1939. Smetacek managed to escape to Hamburg, where he hired a cargo ship. When this docked in Calcutta shortly before the outbreak of World War II, he withdrew.

When the war intensified in Southeast Asia, and Calcutta became the British center of operations, he moved to the city. He found a job in the Bata shoe factory, not least because he shared his Czech origins with company founder Thomas Bata. He had built a whole factory town called Batanagar outside of Calcutta. He ran three companies providing logistical support to the Allies.

In 1941 Smetacek met a young lady, Shahada Ahad, a descendant of Tipu Sultan at a party in Calcutta. Thanks to her aunt Begum Noor -a Russian émigré named Vera Alexandrowa hid behind her name -Shahada was able to leave the strictly guarded women's wing of the Ahad residence every now and then.

After a whirlwind courtship, they married in 1942, and after the war, decided to move to the mountains. They moved to Naukuchiyatal in Kumaon in 1946. After a 5-year stay in the region, they came to Jones Estate, Bhimtal. In 1951, they bought some 1,000 acres in a tea estate dating back to the 1840s, called Jones Estate (named after its last British owner, Colonel Bertram Owen Jones), in partnership with General Madan Shamsher Jung Bahadur Rana and the Rani of Balrampur.

Frederick continued to run the tea estate after he purchased the property but made one change. After two years, he turned the estate bungalow into a guesthouse, aptly naming it 'The Retreat', which became a huge draw for guests from the diplomatic community in Delhi craving for a taste of home. A dilapidated house in a small high valley in the Himalayan foothills. India's largest butterfly collection resides there -and a story of two migrations.

My curious journey to know about the fate of Adolf Hitler started after reading interesting articles about Fred Smetacek.

World War II was reaching a conclusion, and Nazi Germany was being crushed in the conflict it began. The Allies on one side and the Soviet Union on the other were quickly progressing towards Berlin. Hitler's fantasies had now transformed into bad dreams. In this climate, the Soviet chief Stalin provided the accompanying request to the death group SMERSH, which comprised of the most gifted specialists of the KGB; I need Hitler, in any condition! Notwithstanding, this request couldn't be done.

Partnered troops arriving in Normandy entered Germany from the west, and the Soviet Association from the east, and was progressing towards the capital, Berlin. Nazi Germany, which had united the entire world for a wiped-out philosophy, was crushed. Hitler was left with just a single choice. That choice was to end it all before he needed to deal with any consequences regarding his activities or end up like his close buddy Mussolini.

Later billions of projectiles shot all through The Second Great War, the main slug that emerged from Hitler's own weapon was the mark of the story. On April 30, 1945, in his shelter in Berlin, Hitler, getting fresh insight about how Germany was being looted from the two sides, resigned to his room in the fortification, taking his significant other, Eva Braun, with him. To begin with, Hitler's given love Eva broke the cyanide case. The case, that broke in the mouth, produced results in no time, the last passing Hitler saw was the demise of his significant other. It's his move. He broke the cyanide case in his mouth and discharged a shot in the head with his gun to get his work.

Hitler was dead; however, his orders were as yet incomplete. He had requested that his body be incinerated so Stalin would not have toys or whatever was at the forefront of his thoughts. Hitler's last request was done, similar to each and every other request, and just later his demise, the assortments of Adolf Hitler and Eva Braun were incinerated someplace close to the dugout.

Multi-week later Hitler's passing, Germany officially gave up, and the Hub Powers experienced an outright loss. For those left behind, the time had come to clean up, plan for new conflicts and rebuff the blameworthy. The inquiry that the entire world was hanging tight for a response to was: Germany was crushed, however where was this man called Hitler?

Excitedly going to Berlin to complete Stalin's organization, Soviet specialists had the option to observe Hitler's incinerated body. However, did this cadaver, consumed to the point of being unrecognizable, truly have a place with Hitler? There must be a method for discovering. Soviet specialists were scanning each edge of Berlin for the specialist who treated Hitler's teeth. At the point when they observed the dental specialist, they quickly contrasted Hitler's dental and jawbone records and the jawbone they had taken from the consumed body. Indeed, the records were coordinated. Thus, Hitler was dead. It is reputed that Hitler's jawbone is as yet put away in a document in Moscow. The dugout in Berlin, where Hitler ended it all, was exploded by the Soviet armed force. Surprisingly, the Soviet Association didn't impart any data on this issue to general society for quite a long time. Therefore, Hitler's bad dream proceeded for Europe. There was an exceptionally enormous crowd who accepted that he was not dead. He is affirmed to have been seen in a town in Norway one day, one more day living on a ranch in the Alps, or disappearing to Argentina by submarine.

For what reason was the Soviet's information on Hitler's demise kept a mystery for such countless years? For what reason did the Soviet Association want to conceal something like this? That is the unanswered inquiry in the story. It is this unanswered inquiry that takes care of all the paranoid notions on "Hitler escaped", which have effectively arrived at the current day.

What if Hitler was alive after death? A theory is evolving that Netaji's INA men probably helped Hitler take his final refuge to India, where he breathed his last in Kashmir.

TheSmetacek family of Czech descent still runs the homestay called 'The Retreat' -the 150-year-old estate bungalow at Bhimtal, Uttarakhand. I wanted to know whether Hitler really escaped to India and took shelter somewhere in the Himalayan Valley, where he breathed his last. I dropped a mail to Padmini Smetacek to know if any clues Frederick Smetacek left behind regarding Hitler's death or escape. I got her reply within a few days. She has never heard of this interesting theory before.

Somdev Chattopadhyay
17-03-2022

Acknowledgements

https://www.historyextra.com/period/second-world
https://www.thebritishacademy.ac.uk/podcasts
https://julac.hosted.exlibrisgroup.com/primo
https://zimsen.kiwix.campusafrica.gos.orange.com
https://www.theguardian.com/world/2013/oct
https://bigthink.com/culture-religion/forensic
https://www.inverse.com/article/45074-hitler-death
https://www.thedailybeast.com/conspiracy-theorist
https://www.commentary.org/articles/h-trevor-roper
https://www.storytel.com/se/sv/books/hitler-s-death
https://nypost.com/2018/09/04/book-claims-to-have
https://www.deccanchronicle.com/world/europe
https://www.dailymail.co.uk/news/article-6790885
http://www.owlapps.net/owlapps_apps/articles?id
https://www.thetimes.co.uk/article/hitler-conspiracy
https://allthatsinteresting.com/how-did-hitler-diec
https://www.bbc.com/news/world-europe-46964928
https://www.express.co.uk/news/weird/455810
https://en.wikipedia.org/wiki/Conspiracy_theories
https://tricycle.org/magazine/hitler-and-himalayas
https://kashmirobserver.net/2015/06/29/hitler
https://www.afr.com/world/europe/german-nazi
https://studybuddhism.com/en/advanced-studies
https://www.himalmag.com/dalai-lamas-friend
https://link.springer.com/chapter/10.1057
http://www.historymatters.group.shef.ac.uk/delight
https://historyofyesterday.com/declassified-cia-files
https://www.archives.gov/-records/rg-263-report
https://taskandpurpose.com/history/cia-document
https://indianexpress.com/article/opinion/web-edits
https://www.thehindu.com/features/magazine
https://culture.pl/en/article/the-maharaja-who-saved

ACKNOWLEDGEMENTS

https://www.bbc.com/news/world-asia-41662588
https://www.thestatesman.com/opinion/kashmirs
http://www.scoopnews.in/det.aspx?q=99837
https://www.dailysabah.com/americas/2017/09/08
https://www.independent.co.uk/news/world/americas
https://www.businessinsider.com/declassified-fbi-files
https://www.scribd.com/document/292962306
https://www.newsobserver.com/news/nation-world
https://www.mirror.co.uk/news/weird-news/cia-veteran
https://www.muckrock.com/news/archives/2017/sep
https://fpif.org/the_cias_worstkept_secret_newly
https://www.history.com/shows/hunting-hitler/cast
https://www.nytimes.com/2021/04/05/world/europe
https://www.express.co.uk/news/world/1088876
https://sgp.fas.org/eprint/wolfe.pdf
https://forward.com/fast-forward/386508/did-hitler
https://www.theguardian.com/world/2005/may/02
https://www.smh.com.au/world/europe/french-researchers
https://www.historyhit.com/what-are-the-main-conspiracy
https://www.grandforksherald.com/4449135-scientists
https://www.npr.org/2014/11/05/361427276/how
https://www.jpost.com/arts-and-culture/entertainment
https://foreignpolicy.com/2015/04/28/did-the-brutal
https://www.express.co.uk/news/weird/455810
https://scholar.umw.edu/cgi
https://www.the-tls.co.uk/articles/finding-the-fuhrer
https://gizmodo.com/hitlers-secret-argentine-sanctuary
https://timesofindia.indiatimes.com/india/tomb-raider
https://www.greaterkashmir.com/more/the-myth-of
https://www.speakingtree.in/allslides/was-jesus-christ
https://www.oshonews.com/2016/09/24/jesus-in
https://www.reuters.com/article/us-india-jesus-shrine
https://www.washingtonpost.com/history/2019/04/20
https://www.thoughtco.com/hitler-pictures-1779647
Daniel Berehulak/Staff/Getty Images News/Getty Images

ACKNOWLEDGEMENTS

https://english.newsnationtv.com/india/news/netaji
https://www.deccanchronicle.com/world/europe
https://www.vox.com/2014/11/13/7148855/40-maps
https://www.independent.co.uk/news/world/europe
https://www.dw.com/en/former-nurse-tells-of-hitlers-last
https://www.newyorker.com/culture/cultural-comment
https://www.washingtonpost.com/wpsrv/style/longterm
https://www.history.co.uk/article
https://argentinapaiscorrupto.blogspot.com/2013/04
http://www.jewworldorder.org/hitler-escaped-to-argentina
http://timesofindia.indiatimes.com/articleshow
https://timesofindia.indiatimes.com/india/govt-draws-up
https://www.newsclick.in/why-jaitley-needs-study-link
https://kreately.in/hitler-called-it-hooked-cross-church
https://adilmohammedblog.wordpress.com/2015/11/05
http://www.insafbulletin.net/archives/3743
http://www.kashmirtimes.com/newsdet.aspx?q=109061
https://www.express.co.uk/news/world/1494579/adolf
https://studybuddhism.com/en/advanced-studies
https://www.outlookindia.com/outlooktraveller/explore
https://factlo.com/the-indus-valley-civilisation-and-the
https://theprint.in/pageturner/excerpt/aryans-did-not
https://hindutvawatch.org/gurujis-lie-the-rss-and-ms
https://swarajyamag.com/books/even-as-it-stops-short
https://www.google.co.in/books/edition/Hitler
https://en.wikipedia.org/wiki/Indian_National_Army
https://www.dw.com/en/germanys-india-envoy-visits
https://shradhanjali.com/profile/keshav-hedgewar-45
https://discover.hubpages.com/education/The-Submarine
https://www.dnaindia.com/analysis/column-netaji-s
https://www.vedanta.com/store/Abhedananda_journey
https://belurmath.org/holy-lives/swami-abhedananda
https://pdfcoffee.com/jesus-died-in-kashmir
http://www.deinayurveda.net/wordpress/2010/04
http://www.knskashmir.com/totally-wrong-that-jesus-is

ACKNOWLEDGEMENTS

https://timesofindia.indiatimes.com/world/rest-of-world
https://en.wikipedia.org/wiki/F%C3%BChrerbunker
https://en.wikipedia.org/wiki/Roza_Bal
https://archive.org/details/HeirApparentAnAutobiography
https://en.wikipedia.org/wiki/Mai_Mari_da_Ashtan
https://lifestyle.livemint.com/how-to-lounge/books
https://www.youtube.com/watch?v=jo7nE2g1e78
https://www.cntraveller.in/story/places-to-stay
https://www.newindianexpress.com/lifestyle/travel
https://lbb.in/delhi/Colonial-bunglow-Fredy's-Nanital
https://www.traffickingmatters.com/on-this-day-in
https://www.thebetterindia.com/269902/retreat-bhimtal
https://negnews.in/index.php/2021/08/28/bhimtals
https://www.birdsnbeestravel.com/birds-watching
https://onlinereadfreenovel.com/bruce-chatwin
http://www.allwhatshewants.com/2013/05/31
https://www.journal21.ch/artikel/peter-smetacek
https://en.wikipedia.org/wiki/Nicolas_Notovitch
https://en.wikipedia.org/wiki/Mirza_Ghulam_Ahmad
https://en.wikipedia.org/wiki/Jesus_in_Ahmadiyya
https://en.wikipedia.org/wiki/Pahari_people_(Kashmir)
https://en.wikipedia.org/wiki/Hunting_Hitler
https://en.wikipedia.org/wiki/Hunting_Hitler
https://twitter.com/James1940/status
https://zeenews.india.com
https://thewire.in/history
https://www.dailystar.co.uk
https://kashmirthunder.com
https://www.scoopwhoop.com
https://newsriveting.com
https://listamaze.com
https://www.haaretz.com
https://mungfali.com
https://www.tripadvisor.in
https://www.thefreelibrary.com

ACKNOWLEDGEMENTS

https://tricycle.org/magazine
https://www.theguardian.com
https://www.abc.net.au
https://www.timesofisrael.com
https://www.ft.com
https://www.indiatoday.in
https://www.riotimesonline.com
https://www.businessinsider.com.
https://revolutionarydemocracy.org
https://www.cambridge.org
https://go.gale.com
https://www.historyindia.com
https://timesofindia.indiatimes.com
https://books.google.co.in/books
https://rarehistoricalphotos.com
https://thewire.in
https://caravanmagazine.in
https://www.dw.com
https://theprint.in
https://www.trtworld.com
https://www.bbc.com
https://www.haaretz.com
https://www.dnaindia.com
https://timesofindia.indiatimes.com
https://www.news18.com
https://www.wordie.in
https://archive.org
https://www.indiatoday.in
http://www.kashmirtimes.in
https://scroll.in
https://inshorts.com
https://2001-2009.state.gov
https://www.cbsnews.com
https://www.thesun.co.uk
https://indianexpresss.in

ACKNOWLEDGEMENTS

https://timesofindia.indiatimes.com
https://www.unitingearth.com
https://www.ibtimes.com
https://culanth.org
https://edtimes.in/culture
https://www.iflscience.com
https://militaryhistorynow.com
http://jayasreepatrika.org

'*The Lost Years of Jesus: Documentary Evidence of Jesus' 17year Journey to the East*' by Elizabeth Clare Prophet
'*The Last Days of Hitler*' by Hugh Trevor Roper
'*Jesus in India*' by Hadrat Mirza Ghulam Ahmad
'*Kashmir o Tibbote*' by Swami Abhedananda
'*Oi Mahanab Ase*' by Charanik (Akhaṇḍa sanskaraṇa)
'*Oi Mahanab Ase*' by Charanik (Asesa sanskaraṇa)

Prologue

Many sources claim that Adolf Hitler didn't die in his underground Berlin bunker on 30th April 1945 adding to a long list of death conspiracy theories. There are several top conspiracy theories on Adolf Hitler's death. Adolf Hitler was surrounded by many secrets and conspiracy theories during his period of dictatorship and now it continues even after his death. FBI claims that Hitler didn't commit suicide and DNA tests conducted on the skull of Hitler provide evidence that the skull was not of Hitler's but a woman in her 40s. Another source claims that Hitler escaped to Argentina with his wife Eva Braun.

There are many crazy conspiracy theories behind his suicide as well. Some of them include Hitler taking cyanide to kill himself; Hitler shooting himself from his mouth and so on. Though we know that Hitler was one of the cruelest dictator histories that have ever seen, and officially his death was cruel as well. Officially, Hitler died on 30 April 1945 in his Berlin underground Führer bunker by committing suicide.

Here are the top 10 conspiracy theories regarding the death of Adolf Hitler and some of the deadly conspiracy secrets.

1. Hitler Commits Suicide by Hitting Rounds of Bullets in his Berlin Bunker

This is perhaps the actual story of Hitler's death. On April 30, 1945, Adolf Hitler reportedly committed suicide by hitting rounds of bullets in his underground bunker. Hitler killed himself along with his wife Eva who took cyanide to die. The couple lived around 40 hours together in the bunker before taking their lives. As per prior instructions from Hitler, the bodies of Hitler and his wife were set alight with petrol outside the bunker in Reich Chancellery Garden. The burnt remains are archived in the Soviet archives until 1970 after which the ashes were scattered, exhumed, and cremated multiple times. A study conducted in 2009 by American researchers has revealed that the 4-inch bullet-punctured skull is not of Hitler's but a woman's skull in her 40s. There are also many different variations of Hitler's death, such as death by taking cyanide, by taking poison, and so on. There is no proper full-proof evidence that Hitler was burned outside the Reich Chancellery Garden.

2. Hitler Escaped Berlin Bunker and Died in South America at the age of 95

A book claims with pictures that Hitler escaped his underground Berlin bunker and died in South America in 1984 at the age of 95. Hitler is believed to have escaped Germany and lived in a small town near Brazil and the border of Bolivia with his girlfriend Cutinga. Cutinga was a black woman with whom Hitler is believed to have had a relationship. The author also believes that Hitler went to Brazil in search of hidden treasures. The book, titled *Hitler in Brazil –His Life and His Death* 'challenges the views that Hitler shot himself in the Berlin bunker after Germany lost World War II. The book is authored by Simoni Renee Guerreiro Dias.

3. Alleged escape to Argentina

A book called *Grey Wolf: The Escape of Adolf Hitler* by two British authors Simon Dunstan and Gerrard Williams proposes that Hitler and his wife Braun escaped from Berlin to Argentina, and they didn't commit suicide. According to the book, Hitler crossed Andes Mountain before arriving in Argentina. Until the early 1960s, Hitler was in hiding at Hacienda San Ramón. But according to historians, this theory is just considered as another conspiracy theory of Adolf Hitler's death and has no place in historical research. The couple then died of old age in Argentina. Since many Nazis escaped to South American nations, which tends to support the fact that Hitler did the same. Adolf Hitler's secret hideouts have been found in South America. Many Nazi coins have been found in Adolf Hitler's secret hideouts in South America.

4. Fake Hitler Dies in Berlin

On the 70th death anniversary of Hitler on April 30, 2015, again the conspiracy theories on his death were questioned. According to the *New York Times* dated 26th April 1945, entitled *'Hitler Imitator Reported Ready to Die in His Place'*, which speaks of a former grocer, August Wilhelm Bartholdi, who was a double for Hitler and who was thought to be preparing to die on the Fuhrer's behalf, allowing Hitler's end to be faked for posterity. As per a few pieces of evidence and reports that Hitler faked his death and fled to Argentina with Braun and died of old age in Argentina. There is proof from Nazi experts that Hitler lived till the 1960s. This is one of the most famous conspiracy theories on the death of Adolf Hitler.

5. Hitler Buried in Kashmir

This is something recent and this conspiracy theory came in 2015 from Kashmir's noted writer, historian, and former bureaucrat, Farooq Renzu Shah. Further, the writer believes that Hitler was introduced to the then Maharaja of Kashmir by freedom fighter Subhas Chandra Bose's Azad Hind Fauj. Additionally, he believes that Hitler breathed his last in Kashmir and is buried in an unknown grave in Rozabal. According to Shah, the grave is titled Yasuh (Jesus) in Rozabal and rumors are that the grave is of Jesus to keep it as a highly guarded secret. Shah also added that the latest revelation from the British Author Gerrard Williams about the escape of Hitler adds more authenticity to the fact.

6. Hitler Escaped to Outer space with Aliens

An Iranian news agency claims that the aliens helped Hitler and the Nazis. The news agency *Fars News Agency* alleges that The Nazis were controlled by Aliens before and now they are controlling the U.S Government with the alien base in Nevada. In fact, even before World War II, Edgar Rice Burroughs satirized the Nazis by placing a fascist political faction called "Zanis" on the planet Venus in *Carson of Venus*, published in serialized form in 1938.

7. Hitler had Secretly Escaped to Moon

The theme of the Nazis escaping into outer space was even evident in the book *Rocket Ship Galileo* by Robert A. Heinlein. The book was published two years after World War II, which says that the Nazis colonized the moon. Additionally, the Nazis had a secret moon base and Hitler was sent to the moon using rocket technologies. According to a few conspiracy theories from the book, after World War II, Hitler not only escaped his country but escaped from the planet and lived in an underground lunar base.

8. Hitler died of Parkinson's Disease

Parkinson's disease is the main reason behind the downfall of Hitler's claims a few reports. The symptoms of Parkinson's disease include trembling of arms and legs, stiffness in muscles, and slowness of movement. Parkinson's disease is a degenerative disorder that affects the nervous system. It affects the patient slowly and can ultimately lead to death due to secondary complications from the disease. Hitler is known to have suffered the disease for 10 years. Dr. Tom Hutton, a neurologist said Hitler was suffering physical and mental symptoms of the disease, but his aides kept it secret. The declining health of the dictator might have led to his downfall and also his death. This is again one of the conspiracy theories that are still unproven.

9. Hitler Escaped to an Arctic or Antarctica base

There are reports that Antarctica was a Nazi base before World War II, but the South Pole also has locations that are known to be secret bases of the Nazis. But, while tales of a secret Nazi base in Antarctica may appear plausible to some, the idea that a warm water location at the South Pole has remained undiscovered and no one has escaped or deserted the place in more than 50 years stretched belief to the breaking point in years past. But with the new revelations of 60–70-degree temperature water, magnetic anomalies suggesting the possibility of a hidden city or base, and the obvious backout taking place concerning current events at the pole, the idea of a secret base is no longer so far-fetched.

There are also reports that Nazis had a secret base in the North Pole or the Arctic region. Nazis used this secret base to test their flying saucers. During the 1940s, the Nazi government was successful enough to create three flying saucer prototype models, namely Feuerball ("Fireball"), Feuerflaggen ("Fire Flag"), and

Feuerfazzen ("Fire Go").

These pieces of evidence support the point that Hitler might have escaped to an Arctic or Antarctica base.

10. Hitler Escaped and Died in Spain

There are already many claims that Hitler escaped to Spain in a plane. Hitler escaped with General Franco, who took him in. According to Senor Stefan Aceituna (General Franco's driver), he was sent to meet a plane arriving at Madrid airport on the night of April 30, 1945. A different angle of the story is a man living in Venezuela claiming that Hitler is buried in Spain. The man who claims that Hitler is buried in Spain is a Spanish sculptor, composer, writer, and historian. According to the man Hitler never committed suicide but died and was buried in a cemetery in Galicia, northwest Spain.

CHAPTER ONE

Looking at Adolf Hitler's Last Days

"Make the lie big, make it simple, keep saying it, and eventually, they will believe it." -Adolf Hitler

Stars and Stripes from May 2, 1945 -a publication of the US military

A Time Magazine cover from 1945 -One of the most iconic covers of all time

New York Daily News from May 2, 1945

The Daily Express from May 2, 1945, UK

SOMDEV CHATTOPADHYAY

The Salt Lake Tribune from May 2, 1945

Hitler 'Death' Seen as Surrender Evasion

By Louis P. Lochner
Chief of the former Associated Press bureau in Berlin

WITH THE U. S. SEVENTH ARMY, May 1 (/P)—I have just listened to the short-wave broadcast of Adm. Karl Doenitz' speech as the new fuehrer of Germany, but I still find it difficult to believe that Hitler is really dead, or that he even remained in Berlin during the Russian assault upon the capital.

The whole melodramatic build-up beginning with Paul Joseph Goebbels' announcement days ago that Hitler personally was conducting the defense of the capital now reaching its climax in the claim that he met death in the chancellery of all places, looks like an effort to make good der fuehrer's oft-repeated assertion: "I'll never capitulate."

Hitler couldn't afford to accept unconditional surrender, so what may prove to be the legend of his meeting a hero's death had to be staged.

Hitler may or may not be dead. If he is dead, it seems extremely unlikely he died as the German radio says he did. Having spent the past days in the very section of the country where Hitler rose to power, wrote "Mein Kampf," and conducted affairs of intrigue with the whole world from Munich, I still cannot escape the feeling that Hitler is some place where nobody expects him to be.

Bulletin

SAN FRANCISCO, May 2 (INS)—Allied forces in Burma landed on both sides of the Rangoon river south of the city of Rangoon early Wednesday morning, southeast Asia command communique reported.

From time to time people will claim to have seen him. The Doenitz announcement by no means ends our troubles with Hitler. They may only have begun. There may be a state funeral in Berlin, and photographers may be given the opportunity to produce pictures of a dead man labeled Hitler. Then, some day much later, a "resurrected" Hitler may again stir the world.

The appointment of Doenitz as Hitler's successor indicates the nazi leadership desires someone as chief of state who possibly can negotiate with the allies. Doenitz had no real experience in government, and has no real hold on the affections of the German people. His appointment obviously was a political maneuver.

The course of the war is unlikely to be affected by his appointment.

The Tribune seemed especially sceptical of reports of Hitler's death. It refers to the leader's "'death' site" in quotation marks, and lower on the page, it ran an editorial from Associated Press Berlin correspondent Louis Lochner: "I still find it difficult to believe that Hitler is really dead," he wrote.

"Hitler couldn't afford to accept unconditional surrender, so what may prove to be the legend of his meeting a hero's death had to be staged," he went on. "I still cannot escape the feeling that Hitler is in some place where nobody expects him to be."

Hamburger Zeitung from May 1, 1945 - Germany

SHAEF from May 2, 1945 -a newspaper for displaced Allied military members in Europe

El Universo from May 2, 1945 -Ecuador, South America

CHAPTER TWO

ADOLF HITLER'S LAST WITNESS

The Memoirs of Hitler's Bodyguard is being republished by Frontline Books in English on 30th May 2017.

The bodyguard who was the first to lay eyes on Adolf Hitler's dead body has described the last minutes of the Fuhrer's life in intimate detail.

Rochus Misch's autobiography explains how the Nazi leader said all soldiers were "released" from loyalty and that he wanted his body to be burned, before killing himself.

Mr. Misch, who was the last surviving member of Hitler's entourage when he died in Berlin aged 96 in 2013, also described how he walked in on mistress Eva Braun in a "flimsy nightie".

The telephone operator was on the switchboard in Hitler's bunker on 30 April, 1945, when General Keitel messaged in to say the army failed to break the Soviet encirclement in Berlin and that the end of the Second World War was inevitable.

"Shortly afterward, Misch heard Hitler talking quietly to [Nazi party official, Martin] Bormann and others. He looked and saw Hitler walk into his study. Eva, now Mrs Hitler, followed him in," said the book's commissioning editor Martin Mace.

"He saw Otto Günsche, the Führer's adjutant, close the door behind the newly-married couple. Güsche told Misch that the boss was not to be disturbed.

"Hitler shook hands with Günsche and told him that all soldiers were released from their oath of loyalty.

"Hitler had already told his adjutant that he did not want his body to be publicly abused as Mussolini's had been and that he wanted his corpse to be burned."

He added: "Everyone in the bunker waited nervously. Then there was some commotion. The study door was opened and Misch looked inside."

Mr. Misch said: "My glance fell first on Eva. She was seated with her legs drawn up; her head inclined towards Hitler. Her shoes were under the sofa. Near her ... the dead Hitler. His eyes were open and staring, his head had fallen forward slightly."

The memoirs also describe how Mr. Misch walked in on Eva in a "flimsy nightie" in the guestroom, which had a private passageway into Hitler's room, and she put a finger to her mouth telling the bodyguard to keep quiet.

Mr. Misch, who thought he would be sacked over the incident, also said he heard Ms. Braun and Magada Goebbels swearing to die with their respective men. Mr. Misch was kidnapped by the Soviet Red Army, and imprisoned in labor camps for eight years, after trying to escape into hiding.

He spoke fondly of Hitler until his later years, describing him as a "wonderful boss" and "no brute", and was thought to be the last survivor of the Führerbunker after Siegfried Knappe died in December 2008. The Holocaust Memorial Trust declined to comment.

Frontline Books senior editor John Grehan said Mr. Misch's account is remarkably impartial and non-judgemental.

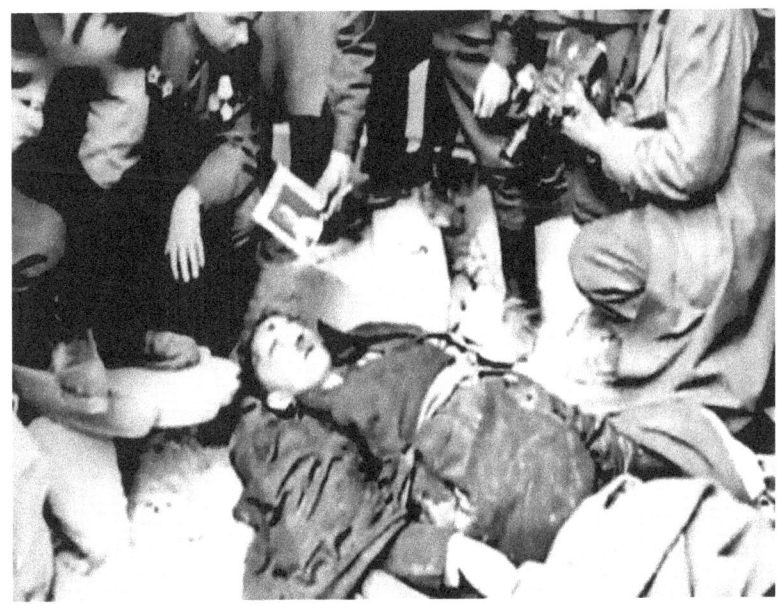

CHAPTER THREE

Adolf Hitler's Last Days

A 93-year-old woman claiming to have been Adolf Hitler's nurse in the final days of the Third Reich has spoken of her experiences in the Berlin bunker for the first time in 60 years.

Did Paranoia paralyze Hitler in the end?

Many people have tried and failed to accurately portray or document the final hours of Adolf Hitler. Acclaimed attempts such as the recent successful German film "Der Untergang" (The Downfall) have made the most of the knowledge which is available and have mixed established facts and speculation to great effect.

But there have been very few corroborative first-hand accounts that have revealed the true inner workings of the Führer's bunker and his mindset as his master plan came crashing down around him.

Until now, possibly. According to the Berlin-based daily *Berliner Zeitung,* a survivor from Hitler's Berlin stronghold has decided to break her silence over what she saw and heard in the final days of the Third Reich.

Erna Flegel, a 93-year-old, claims to have been the Nazi leader's nurse at the end of World War II and to have been in his bunker when Hitler took his own life.

Under the headline "I was Hitler's nurse", Flegel tells a fascinating and tragic story of how she provided medical treatment to Hitler and his inner circle from 1943 until the Nazi leadership gave up their dogged resistance and hope in the face of the advancing Red Army and Allied forces two years later.

Flegel's insight into the last days reveals that contemporary accounts have been more or less accurate concerning the mental state of the Führer.

Adolf Hitler didn't even trust his own cyanide capsules at the end

The former nurse revealed in the interview that Hitler was almost paralyzed with paranoia as the end neared, even fearing that the cyanide capsules with which he was planning to take his own life had been switched and filled with fake poison. "By the end, he didn't trust anyone anymore -not even the cyanide capsule he swallowed," she is quoted as saying in the paper.

Conflicting reports suggest that only Hitler's wife Eva took cyanide while the Nazi leader himself died from a self-inflicted gunshot to the head. Both bodies were allegedly burned by aides shortly after being discovered.

After Hitler committed suicide, Flegel stayed in the bunker as the Nazi regime crumbled around her. Flegel said that after Hitler's suicide, Josef Goebbels, the Nazi propaganda chief, took over as leader, but by then there was little sense of command, and Goebbels was ignored.

A witness to the desperate end of the Third Reich

She also revealed her desperate attempts to save Goebbels' six children from Magda, their "merciless" mother, but was ultimately powerless as she poisoned them. It was then that the Nazi hierarchy within the bunker began to implode.

"(Hitler's) last subordinates shot themselves in succession," she said. "And those who didn't shoot themselves tried to flee." Still, Flegel remained underground. "I had to look after the wounded," she added.

Red Army approach heralded the final collapse

In the interview, she remembers the approach of the Soviet Army and the realization that Hitler's brutal regime and his plans for world domination were ending in the dust and rubble of Berlin above. "You could feel that the Third Reich was coming to an end," she said. "The radios stopped working and it was impossible to get information."

She recalled that the Russians treated her well and advised her to remain where she was and to keep the door closed and locked. Flegel stayed for several more days in the bunker and was one of the last to leave. She was then interviewed by US secret service agents, the last time that she spoke about her life as Hitler's nurse until now.

"I don't want to take my secret with me to the grave," she said.

According to a report in The Guardian in 2005, a German film on Hitler's death has freed one old soldier to tell his story at last.

After nine months in Adolf Hitler's bunker, with Berlin about to fall, Bernd Freytag von Loringhoven was allowed to leave.

'As Hitler shook my hand and wished me luck, I saw a glint of envy in his eye,' says the 91-year-old former Wehrmacht aide-de-camp. A day later, on 30 April 1945, Hitler was dead, and the terrified soldier was in a canoe on Havel River, dodging Soviet shelling, trying to reach the last German-held position in Berlin. Sixty years on, he believes a 'legion of guardian angels' spared him death at the hands of the Soviets, of fanatical Nazis, and of 'primitive sentries' who tortured him in a British prisoner-of-war camp.

Today Baron Freytag von Loringhoven is the only survivor among the close advisers of the Führer -who he says was probably a drug addict. For many years a Germany steeped in guilt did not want to hear his story. Now it has taken a French publisher, Perrin, to release Dans le Bunker de Hitler - his unique account of the days leading up to the suicide of the Führer and his wife Eva Braun. The baron also helped the makers of the film Downfall, which charts Hitler's end and opens in British cinemas on Friday.

A nobleman from the Baltic states, Freytag von Loringhoven was viewed with suspicion by the Nazis 'who loathed education, real culture, and tradition'. Unlike Hitler's secretary, Traudl Junge, whose memoirs were published before her death two years ago, he claims he never fell under the Führer's spell and insists the distinction between the professional Wehrmacht and politicised Waffen-SS was real. 'After the war, I had the unpleasant feeling of having served as a combustible, as heating wood, for the adventures of a charlatan,' he says. 'I had served a criminal regime while remaining loyal to my military convictions.' It was only as a prisoner of war that he realised the Nazis had murdered Jews 'on an industrial scale', he says. 'We didn't even know the names of the concentration camps.'

In the bunker, Freytag von Loringhoven observed Hitler divide and rule among sycophants and soldiers. 'He created parallel command structures that competed for resources, and he appointed political officers to spy on military professionals. Right until the end, he kept all the cards in his hand.

'Hitler's only military experience had been as a corporal during the First World War. He knew only one thing -the 'fanatischer widerstand' (fanatical resistance), and I can still hear him say the words. Blitzkrieg was not devised by him but by military strategists whom he later sidelined. As soon as we suffered the first setbacks, he became deaf to calls to switch to modern, mobile defense techniques. He saw them as defeatists since they sometimes required giving up territory.

'Hitler could be very aggressive but towards the end, he was very controlled. He could be pleasant and even warm. He could be very charming -he was a real Austrian. People were impressed when he asked them questions about their lives. It was a way of controlling them. He played with people.'

Hitler swore by his doctor, Theodor Morell, a charlatan who gave him glucose injections and stimulants. 'Morell made a lot of money during the war, not least with a louse powder we were given on the eastern front which smelt awful and was useless.' The baron holds Morell in particular contempt: 'I shall never forget how he begged, on 22 and 23 April, when the women were allowed to leave. He sat there like a fat sack of potatoes and begged to fly out. And he did.'

For the last few months of the war, Hitler lived in the fetid air of the bunker, concealed beneath eight meters of concrete, occasionally going outside to play with his dog.

'Hitler got up at around midday. The main event was the afternoon meeting on the military situation. It would be announced, "Meine Herren, der Führer kommt", and everyone made the Nazi salute. Hitler entered the room, shook everyone's hand - it was a limp handshake - and sat down. He was the only one allowed to sit at the map table, which he adored because he was obsessed by detail, and occasionally made concessions to older officers, allowing them to sit on a stool.'

Freytag von Loringhoven, a tall, elegant man with thin bands of gold on the little finger of his left hand and a tweed jacket that looks tailor-made, albeit some time ago, served at Stalingrad. 'I had studied law, but the profession was being taken over by the Nazis. My family had been ruined and I had no way of buying my independence. The Wehrmacht seemed an honourable career.'

Sitting in an armchair in his Munich study, speaking perfect English punctuated by German adjectives, he occasionally reaches into a pile of books to check facts. Maria, the housekeeper who cares for him and his third wife, Herta, 76, has brought coffee. Next to his china cup lie two bound notebooks, marked 'Wartime Log'. In them is an anecdote the baron especially wants Observer readers to hear: 'While I was a prisoner, I met a German counter-intelligence officer. He had been based in Holland and had infiltrated the Dutch resistance movement and learnt the code they used with London. One day he got the idea he wanted a new suit. He sent a message to British intelligence, and they answered, 'OK, what are your measurements?" He sent them, and not long afterward he received a parcel with three Savile Row suits!'

But the British did not treat the baron well after his capture on 13 May 1945. 'My British guards would not believe I was not a Nazi,' he says. 'For three days, from morning until evening, they forced me to clean my cell and scrape paint off tiles with my nails. They kicked me and poured water on me. At the end of the day, they took my wet clothes and forced me to sleep naked on the wet floor.'

After the war, his wife left him, and he was destitute. A friend gave him work in a publishing firm. He married again and his son is now a diplomat at the German embassy in Moscow. In 1956 he returned to a military career and spent three years in Washington DC as a member of NATO's Standing Group. 'I was the only German officer in the planning group of the Atlantic Alliance, reporting to three superiors who were American, British, and French. All had fought against Germany, but my background did not prevent us from becoming firm friends.'

Freytag von Loringhoven agrees with the historical opinion that the Treaty of Versailles, signed after the First World War, was a major cause of the second because it humiliated Germany. But he adds: 'There was more. There was a leader who was like no other man I have ever met.'

CHAPTER FOUR

LIFE IN THE FÜHRERBUNKER

Armin Lehmann, a fanatical, sixteen-year-old member of the Hitler Youth who, along with thousands of teenagers, had been transported to Berlin in early April 1945 to defend the city against the rapidly advancing Red Army. Lehmann was chosen as a courier, running messages backward and forward from the radio room of the Reich Chancellery to and from the diminishing figure of Adolf Hitler. By April, Hitler had permanently retired to an underground bomb shelter located close to the Chancellery known as the Führerbunker. Lehmann was to witness firsthand the final days of the man who had brought Germany to its knees.

The bunker, which consisted of two connected shelters, was completed in stages between 1936 and 1944. Hitler took up residence in the lower bunker with his long-term partner, Eva Braun, and various staff members on the 16th of January 1945. Expensive carpets and rugs covered the floors and artworks taken from the Chancellery lined the walls, including Hitler's favourite painting of Frederick the Great, which hung on the wall above his desk in his comfortable private quarters.

Hitler would spend a total of 105 days living in the bunker. As the net closed in on his regime, life for the staff in both the Chancellery and the bunker descended into drunkenness and decadence. Officers, among them Martin Bormann, Hitler's unpopular brute of a private secretary, often laid into the Chancellery's extensive wine cellar early in the day. A notorious womanizer, Bormann found plenty of takers in the increasingly cavalier atmosphere that took hold as the Soviets closed in.'

Hitler, meanwhile, took daily strolls around the elegant gardens of the Chancellery with his beloved German Shepherd dog, Blondi. It was one of his last remaining pleasures. However, as the Red Army began its final advance on the capital and shells began to rain down on the Chancellery and its gardens, even this was denied him.

The last day Hitler ventured outside was on the morning of April the 20th. It was his 56th birthday. By this stage, he cut a very different figure from the triumphant conqueror of just five years before. Addicted to powerful opiates prescribed to him by his personal physician, Dr. Theodor Morell, visibly shaking from Parkinson's Disease and looking much older than his age, the Führer made his way out to the now ruined Chancellery Garden to hand out medals to children of the Hitler Youth.

As his previously loyal commanders began to desert him, Hitler realised the end of his rule.

Amongst those meeting Hitler that day was Armin Lehmann. He received an Iron Cross from the Führer for bravery during a battle in which he had saved two of his comrades in early January. The boy couldn't believe it when Hitler grabbed him by the cheek and gave his face a playful shake. 'We all idolised Hitler,' he later recalled. "We were dedicated to following his path unerringly even though we were dodging Allied bullets.'

After his brief time outside, Hitler returned to his bunker and never came out again. The following day, he ordered what remained of his forces to attack the advancing Soviets, but his orders were ignored. On hearing this, Hitler flew into a rage and for the first time, he acknowledged the war was lost. It was now only a matter of time before Berlin was overrun and the Soviets reached the Führerbunker.

Six days after realising the war was lost, Hitler received the news that Heinrich Himmler was trying to negotiate Germany's surrender with the Americans. Apoplectic with rage over this betrayal, Hitler declared Himmler a traitor and had his SS representative, the loathsome Hermann Fegelein, taken out and shot. That Fegelein happened to be Eva Braun's brother-in-law made no difference to the furious dictator.

As his previously loyal commanders began to desert him, Hitler realised the end of his rule was nigh. News reached him that Benito Mussolini had been captured, executed and his body hanged upside down from a lamppost in Milan. Determined not to share the same humiliation, Hitler decided to end his life. Eva Braun told Hitler she would die alongside him. For her unerring loyalty, Hitler finally decided to marry her.

The couple were married just after midnight on the 29th of April in a civil ceremony that involved both parties swearing they were of pure Aryan blood. A rather muted wedding reception was held after the ceremony while Hitler retired to his study with his secretary, Traudl Junge, to dictate his last will and testament. In it, he once again blamed the Jews for his and Germany's ills.

The following day, Hitler received word that the troops defending Berlin were rapidly running out of ammunition and it was only a matter of time before the encircling Soviet forces overran the bunker. Hitler realised his time had run out.

'He was like a ghost -he didn't seem to see me or anyone,' Lehmann later recalled. 'He just stared ahead, lost in thought. At that moment, the bunker was shaken by a strong tremor as a bomb hit. Dirt and mortar trickled down on us, but he made no attempt to brush it off. He looked so much unhealthier than 10 days earlier at his birthday reception when I had first met him. It looked like he was suffering from jaundice. His face was sallow.'

After instructing his physician to poison his dog Blondi to test the effectiveness of the cyanide capsules he and Eva intended to take, Hitler and his new bride said their goodbyes to the bunker staff and retired to their private quarters. There, Braun killed herself with cyanide and Hitler shot himself. As per his instructions, Hitler and Braun's bodies were taken out into the

Chancellery garden and burned. Because the grounds of the Chancellery were being almost constantly shelled by this stage, the guard charged with the hasty cremation dashed to the bunker entrance and tossed a lighter at the petrol-soaked bodies. As a result, another guard who had not witnessed this dash to the door thought the bodies had spontaneously combusted.

The couple were married just after midnight on the 29th of April in a civil ceremony that involved both parties swearing they were of pure Aryan blood. A rather muted wedding reception was held after the ceremony while Hitler retired to his study with his secretary, Traudl Junge, to dictate his last will and testament. In it, he once again blamed the Jews for his and Germany's ills.

The following day, Hitler received word that the troops defending Berlin were rapidly running out of ammunition and it was only a matter of time before the encircling Soviet forces overran the bunker. Hitler realised his time had run out.

'He was like a ghost -he didn't seem to see me or anyone,' Lehmann later recalled. 'He just stared ahead, lost in thought. At that moment, the bunker was shaken by a strong tremor as a bomb hit. Dirt and mortar trickled down on us, but he made no attempt to brush it off. He looked so much unhealthier than 10 days earlier at his birthday reception when I had first met him. It looked like he was suffering from jaundice. His face was sallow.'

The following day, Magda Goebbels –who along with her husband Joseph and her six children had moved into the bunker on April 22 –killed her children with the aid of an SS dentist. Goebbels and his wife then ascended into the gardens where they were shot dead or committed suicide (reports vary) and their bodies were burned. Their bodies were not buried but instead left out on the crater-pitted ground to be discovered by Soviet troops two days later.

The remaining staff either committed suicide or made several bloody attempts to break out of the bunker and through the Soviet lines. Some made it out, many others did not. Armin Lehmann managed to evade capture by the Red Army. He was shot during his escape and later captured by American troops who treated his wounds. Martin Bormann was not so lucky. He managed to cross the river Spree, but his body was later seen lying dead on the ground by Hitler Youth leader Artur Axmann as he also made his escape.

The bunker was finally captured by Soviet forces on May 2. Inside, they found the six bodies of Magda Goebbels' murdered children. The bodies of Hitler and Braun were dug up and Hitler was later identified by his dental records. The bodies of Hitler, Braun, Hitler's dogs, and the Goebbels family were buried and exhumed several times before finally being crushed into dust and tossed into the river Elbe in 1970. Nothing now remains of Hitler save for a small section of his jaw and part of his skull.

The bunker was dynamited as part of the demolition of the Reich Chancellery between 1945 and 1949. The dynamite caused some damage, but most of the structure remained intact. Parts of the bunker were demolished when the area was developed in the 1990s, but quite a lot remains and there is now an ongoing debate in Germany over whether it should be opened up to tourists. In the meantime, all that now indicates that this was once the final bolt hole of a grotesque tyrant is a small information board next to a bare patch of ground.

And what of Armin Lehmann, the fanatically loyal teenager who was one of the last people to see Hitler alive? He was forced to witness for himself the monstrousness of the regime he supported when the Americans took him to see the horrors of a Nazi death camp. He renounced his Nazi faith that very same day and decided to become a peace activist. He spent the rest of his life travelling around the world promoting peace, tolerance, and non-violence at events held in over 150 countries. He died in Coos Bay, Oregon on the 10th of October 2008.

CHAPTER FIVE

Delight, Dismay and Disbelief

Caroline Sharples, a Senior Lecturer in Modern European History at the University of Roehampton, writes in the 'History Matters', 30th April 2020: The first formal declaration of Hitler's death came late on the evening of 1 May 1945 via a radio broadcast by Grand Admiral Karl Dönitz. Somber music and drum rolls gave way to the momentous announcement: 'our Führer, Adolf Hitler, has fallen. In the deepest sorrow and respect, the German people bow'. It was, proclaimed Dönitz, a 'hero's death', Hitler falling in battle while fighting valiantly against the 'Bolshevik storm'.

'Hitler Dead' screamed countless international headlines the next day. The bold, dramatic, and matter-of-fact statement left little room for ambiguity. Hitler had met his end; National Socialism was vanquished, and the Second World War was effectively over. The *Daily Herald* printed a caricature of a burning Nazi emblem under the slogan 'WAStika'. The cover of *Time* magazine simply struck Hitler's face out with a large red cross.

The media's response to Hitler's passing was predominantly one of intense relief. 'The whole building cheered', recalled Karl Lehmann, a member of the BBC Monitoring unit. Numerous editorials depicted it as a moment of universal liberation – 'a terrible scourge and force of evil has been removed', declared the *Lancashire Daily Post*. The sense of catharsis continued into the VE

Day celebrations a few days later when the burning of Hitler's effigy typically formed the high point of the UK's festivities.

In the midst of this jubilation, however, there was widespread uncertainty about the precise cause of death. Dönitz's talk of Hitler 'falling' in battle filled the first wave of international news reports, but many of the accompanying editorials urged caution about accepting this at face value. There was suspicion that either the Nazis were exaggerating the circumstances of his demise to foster a 'Hitler legend', or that they were peddling an entirely false narrative to distract from his retreat from the scene. Questioned on the matter during a White House press conference, President Harry S. Truman insisted that he had it 'on the best authority possible' that Hitler was, indeed, dead –but conceded there were no details yet as to *how* he died.

The press was right to question the death-in-battle scenario invented in the Dönitz broadcast. Stationed in Flensburg, over 270 miles away from the death scene, the Admiral was reliant upon information fed to him by colleagues in Führerbunker, namely Propaganda Minister Joseph Goebbels and Head of the Party Chancellery Martin Bormann. The pair had already delayed sending definitive news of Hitler's passing, prompting Dönitz to misdate the fatal moment to the afternoon of 1 May, rather than the 30 April. They also neglected to supply details of what, exactly, had occurred, leaving Dönitz to fill in the gaps for himself. As it transpired, he was not the only person speculating on Hitler's fate.

The Western Allies, anxious to puncture martyrdom myths before they could take hold, swiftly countered Dönitz's heroic imagery by reviving rumours of Hitler's previously failing health. The Soviets, meanwhile, denounced reports of Hitler's death as a 'fascist trick' to conceal his escape from Berlin. Even when reports of a Hitler suicide emerged from 3 May, the debate continued as to whether the Nazi leader had shot himself or taken cyanide -poison being perceived by the Soviets as a particularly cowardly (And thus, eminently appropriate) way out for Hitler.

The United States made propaganda forgery of the Nazi German stamp. Portrait of Hitler made into skull; instead of "German Reich" the stamp reads "Lost Reich". Produced by Operation Cornflakes, U.S. Office of Strategic Services, circa 1942.

What, though, did the general public make of all this? Within hours of the Dönitz broadcast, the *New York Times* and the social research organization Mass Observation were gauging reactions across Manhattan and London respectively. At first, the news appeared anticlimactic; people who had longed for this moment felt disoriented, numb, or empty now it was finally upon them. As the implications sunk in, Hitler's death raised optimism that the war might finally be over, but dashed hopes that the public would see him brought to justice. 'Too bad he's dead', mused one young New

Yorker, 'he should have been tortured'.

The overwhelming reaction to news of Hitler's demise, though, was one of disbelief. Some skeptics perceived the whole affair as a Nazi ruse, with Hitler just waiting to 'pop out again when we aren't looking. Others foreshadowed modern-day accusations of 'fake news', directing their cynicism towards the contradictory explanations printed in the Allied press for Hitler's demise. Mistrust of Nazi propaganda was also, understandably, common with one Londoner reflecting, 'I don't believe he died fighting. They just said that to make it seem more –you know –the way he'd have wanted people to think he died... I think personally he's been out of the way for a long time now.'

Ultimately, the competing versions of Hitler's death ensured that the timing and cause of his demise became quite fluid within the public imagination. This, together with initial Soviet refusals to disclose the recovery of an identifiable corpse outside the bunker, created a vacuum in which all manner of rumours could take root. By contrast, the death of Benito Mussolini was commonly regarded with satisfaction because the deliberate display of his body rendered it an indisputable fact. It was only in 2000 that images of Hitler's jaw (alongside a fragment of skull erroneously attributed to him) were publicly exhibited in Moscow, demonstrating how documenting the truth about his fate has proved a protracted process, and explaining why the Nazi leader has managed to remain so 'alive' in public discussion for all these years.

CHAPTER SIX

MI5: THE HUNT FOR ADOLF HITLER

During World War II, the Security Service MI5, UK played a key role in combating enemy espionage, intercepting German communications, and feeding misinformation back to Germany. According to MI5, in June 1945, the Soviets announced falsely-that Hitler's remains had not been found and that he was probably still alive.

This announcement caused a predictable flurry of "Hitler sightings" across Europe. Allied officers sought to establish beyond possible doubt that Hitler had indeed died in his bunker. To that end, they interrogated various members of Hitler's personal staff who had been with the dictator in late April 1945.

The historian Hugh Trevor-Roper, who served as a British military intelligence officer during the war, used these accounts to investigate the circumstances of Hitler's death and rebut claims that Hitler was still alive and living somewhere in the West. He published an account of his findings in 1947 in his book, *The Last Days of Hitler*.

At the end of the Second World War various members of Hitler's personal staff, who had been with him in the bunker during April 1945, were interrogated by Allied officers seeking to establish beyond possible doubt that Hitler had died. Their questioning concentrated on the events that took place in the Bunker during the last days of April. By then the Red Army had surrounded Berlin and the sound of shellfire could be heard clearly from within the Führerbunker.

Hitler's will and marriage

Hitler retreated to the bunker in January 1945 as the Russians advanced across Poland towards eastern Germany and the Allied airforces devastated Berlin with bombing raids. By the start of April 1945, 2.5 million Russian soldiers had reached the German capital. Two weeks later, they had reached the city center and were fighting within only a few hundred yards of Hitler's refuge.

In the small hours of 28-29 April Hitler dictated his will, in the form of a political and personal testament, to Gertrud "Traudl" Junge, who was one of his secretaries. Soon afterward Hitler and his mistress Eva Braun were married.

Accounts from two of the secretaries present recorded that they had been called together to see the newly married couple. Hitler and Eva emerged from the map-room where the marriage ceremony had taken place, accompanied by Goebbels, his wife Magda, and Hitler's private secretary Martin Bormann. Turning to Hitler's personal secretary, Gerda Christian, Eva pointed to the wedding ring on her finger and received her congratulations.

A party followed to celebrate the occasion. According to Christian, Hitler talked mostly of the past and of happier times. However, he admitted to her that he knew the war was lost. He added that he would never allow himself to be taken prisoner by the Russians but intended to shoot himself. He confided to Junge that the wedding had been an emotional experience, but that for him death would only mean a personal redemption of his many worries and of what had been a very difficult life.

Christian, who was accustomed to joining Hitler and Eva for certain meals, was invited to the wedding breakfast after the ceremony but left early, telling Junge that she had been unable to stand the atmosphere of gloom and despondency.

Preparations for death

On the morning of 29th April, the inhabitants of the bunker received news of the execution by Italian partisans of Mussolini and his mistress, Claretta Petacci. One of those interrogated commented that this would have served to reinforce Hitler's determination that neither he nor Eva Braun should face this fate.

Hitler ordered his staff to prepare for the end. An eyewitness noted that Hitler's SS bodyguards were destroying his personal papers. Elsewhere one of the doctors was instructed by Hitler to poison Blondi, his Alsatian dog, and Eva Braun's spaniel. The eyewitnesses also described how on the afternoon of 29 April Hitler went from room to room shaking hands with all but his immediate staff, saying a few words of encouragement and thanks to each.

By the morning of 30 April, Russian forces had reached the nearby Potsdamer Platz and the sounds of battle were all around. One version on record suggests that Eva was overheard crying, "I would rather die here. I do not want to escape". She and Hitler later emerged from their suite, their personal staff having been assembled, and went around the room shaking hands silently. Everyone knew that the time had come.

Junge recalled that she and Christian both asked Hitler for a poison capsule, having noted the rapid effect that the poison had had on Hitler's dog. Hitler gave them one each, saying as he did so that he was sorry he had no better parting gift and that he wished his generals had been as poised and brave as they were. Eva embraced Junge and, in what seems to have been her last recorded words said, "Take my fur coat as a memory. I always like well-dressed women". Then, saying "It is finished, goodbye", Hitler took

Eva back into their rooms for the last time. During the afternoon Hitler shot himself and Eva took the poison capsule that he had given her.

Disposal of the bodies

Soon afterward their bodies were carried up the stairs to a small garden outside the door to the bunker complex. Hitler's driver, another of those interrogated, helped carry Eva's body some of the ways and noted that once there it was placed on the ground beside Hitler's. He told his interrogators he had noticed that she had been wearing a blue summer dress made of real silk, that her shoes had cork heels, and that her hair was "artificially blonde".

Moments later the same witness saw a party including Goebbels and Bormann gathered beside the bodies. One of them poured petrol from a can over the bodies. They then retired to the safety of a doorway with the sound of Russian artillery all around them. Hitler's adjutant lit a petrol-soaked rag and threw it on the bodies, which immediately burst into flames. The group made the Hitlergruss (the Nazi salute) and withdrew.

One of the bunker guards arrived late on the scene. He described how he was greatly startled to see the two bodies burst into flames as if by spontaneous combustion. He had been unable to see the Goebbels party concealed in a doorway and only later was told the true circumstances.

The bodies were only partly destroyed by the fire and were later hastily buried in a shallow bomb crater. According to Russian reports, the bodies were exhumed by Soviet troops and taken to Magdeburg in East Germany where Hitler's body was said to have been finally destroyed in April 1970 by the KGB. Two fragments of the body, a jawbone, and skull, were preserved. They were displayed in an exhibition at the Russian Federal Archives in Moscow in April 2000.

CHAPTER SEVEN

FBI: Hitler's death in the Führerbunker is questionable

We Are The Mighty by Blake Stilwell in Insider, Jan 22, 2016, reads: Adolf Hitler Screengrab. A recently declassified, heavily redacted FBI field report contains information about Adolf Hitler's alleged escape to Argentina via submarine, which is noteworthy considering that Hitler was reported to have committed suicide in 1945 before the Red Army captured Berlin.

The FBI report dated September 21, 1945, tells the story of a man who aided six top Argentinian officials in landing Hitler onto Argentine soil via submarine and hid him in the foothills of the Andes mountains.

Unfortunately, the report wasn't verifiable at the time because something important couldn't be located. That's not a teaser, the item or person in question is redacted. The document relates the story told to the FBI by a reporter of *The Los Angeles Examiner*.

In July 1945, the reporter's friend "Jack" met with an individual from the Argentine government who wanted to relay a story, but only if he could be guaranteed he wouldn't be sent back to

Argentina, which had just experienced a military coup.

The informant claimed to be one of four men who met Hitler on an Argentine shore about two weeks after the fall of Berlin in 1945, where Hitler and his new wife Eva Braun ostensibly committed suicide.

Soviet records claim the bodies of Hitler and Braun were burned and the remains buried and exhumed repeatedly, making verification difficult.

Hitler supposedly came ashore with 50 or so others and went into hiding in the towns of San Antonio, Videma, Neuquen, Muster, Carmena, and Rason, staying with German families. the informant claimed to remember all six officials and the three other men with him on the shore the night the German fugitive arrived, suffering from asthma and ulcers. Hitler also shaved his signature mustache, revealing a distinct "butt" on his upper lip.

A personal letter to J. Edgar Hoover, the FBI director, was also written by the informant. It mentioned specifically that Hitler lived in an underground residence in Argentina 675 miles West of Florianopolis, 430 miles Northwest of Buenos Aires. The former dictator lived with two body doubles in a secret area behind a photosensitive wall that slid back to reveal the bunker entrance.

Hitler and his inner circle made use of a bank account provided by one "Mrs. Eichorn" who ran a large spa hotel in La Falda, Argentina, to the tune of 30,000 Reichsmarks (just over $2 two million dollars in 2015). Eichorn and her family made repeated visits to Nazi Germany where they would stay with Hitler during their visits.

The informant was paid $15,000 (almost $200,000 adjusted for inflation in 2015) for his help, but he said the matter weighed on his mind too much just to let it go, so he approached the Americans.

He told the reporter's friend to go to a hotel in San Antonio, Argentina, and meet up with a man who would help locate the location of Hitler's ranch, which was heavily guarded. Hitler speaks to Reichminister Joseph Goebbels.

Enter CaptionHitler's Führerbunker. Screengrab/Discovery Channel

The FBI even looked to world news publications, finding photos of famous Argentines, which lends credibility to the idea that high-placed Argentinian officials might help Hitler enter Argentina.

The reporter was to put an ad in the local paper and then call "Hempstead 8458" (these were the days before all-number dialing, which meant that Hempstead was the location of the network and the number is the last four digits of the actual phone number) to let the man know to make proper arrangements.

The informant was unable to shed any more light on the story for the reporter and despite attempts to set up a further meeting, the reporter was unable to contact the informant directly. The FBI watched the diner where the reporter ate his meals to see if "Jack" or the informant ever appeared, to no avail.

Immigration and Naturalization Service (INS) for the names of known aliases for Hitler, Jack, or the informant. The FBI deemed the story credible but didn't have enough information to make a full investigation.

An FBI memorandum to Hoover remarked that the agent in charge of the investigation believed both Hitler and Braun survived the Fall of Berlin. Both their bodies had not been found or identified at the time. He believed they both disappeared the day before the Russians entered Berlin. He believed Hitler's normal relationship with Switzerland along with Hitler's lack of any other language would make Switzerland, not Argentina, the ideal place for the two to escape.

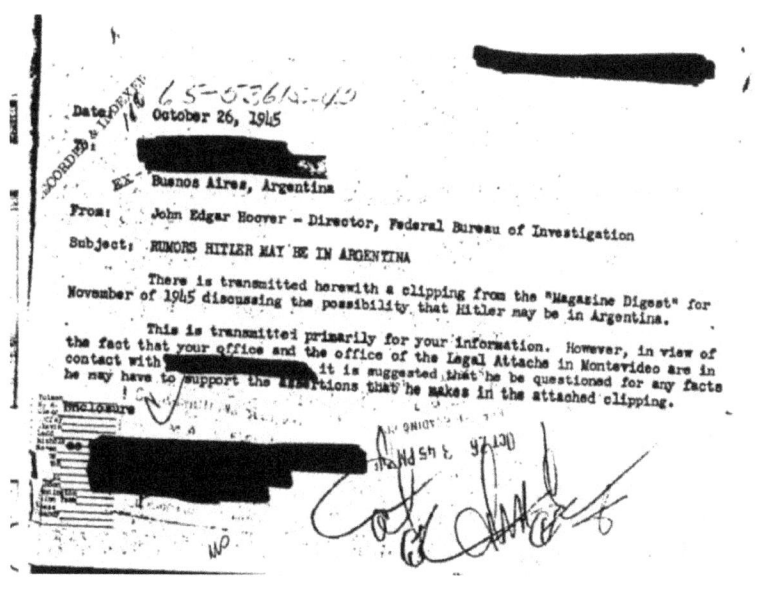

FBI Document

CHAPTER EIGHT

Hitler in Argentina?

A book claims with pictures that Hitler escaped his underground Berlin bunker and died in South America in 1984 at the age of 95. Hitler is believed to have escaped Germany and lived in a small town near Brazil and the border of Bolivia with his girlfriend Cutinga. Cutinga was a black woman with whom Hitler is believed to have had a relationship. The author also believes that Hitler went to Brazil in search of hidden treasures. The book, titled '*Hitler in Brazil –His Life and His Death*' challenges the views that Hitler shot himself in the Berlin bunker after Germany lost World War II. The book is authored by Simoni Renee Guerreiro Dias.

Bob Baer is not alone in this theory. What if this was another distraction while the Führer was actually whisked away in a shadowy plot to ensure he would not fall into the clutches of advancing Soviets? Historian Abel Basti detailed a hypothesis in a new edition of his book published in Argentina, "Hitler in Exile" an account that made headlines, even with such mainstream media like the Huffington Post.

"There was an agreement with the US that Hitler would run away and that he shouldn't fall into the hands of the Soviet Union," Basti said.

"This also applies to many scientists, the military, and spies who later took part in the struggle against the Soviet regime."

Basti believes that Hitler slipped to safety via a tunnel beneath the Chancellery connected to Tempelhof Airport, where a helicopter was waiting to whisk the Dictator to Spain.

Traveling first to the Canary Islands, Hitler made his way to Argentina on a U-boat, where he lived for ten years before settling in Paraguay under the protection of dictator Alfredo Stroessner.

"Wealthy families who helped him over the years were responsible for the organization of his funeral," Basti explained.

"Hitler was buried in an underground bunker, which is now an elegant hotel in the city of Asuncion.

"In 1973, the entrance to the bunker was sealed, and 40 people came to say goodbye to Hitler. One of those who attended [the funeral], Brazilian serviceman Fernando Nogueira de Araujo, then told a newspaper about the ceremony."

In declassified FBI documents, *it is the first-hand account of someone named Guydano who was sent to meet Hitler and his party (fifty people in total) as soon as they landed from submarines in Argentina, two and a half weeks after the fall of Berlin.*

Guydano explained that this affair was arranged by six Argentinian top officials and he was ready to reveal their names as soon as Hitler was caught. He was convinced that it was only a matter of time before Hitler was going to be apprehended and feared that he would be accused of being part of the plot.

Excerpt: "GUYDANO was one of the four men who met Hitler and his party when they landed from submarines in Argentina who and half weeks after the fall of Berlin.

"Hitler... with two women, a doctor, and several other men numbering in or about fifty persons came ashore. (...) at the dusk, the party arrived at the ranch where Hitler and his party are now in hiding.

"According to GUYDANO, this affair was arranged by six top Argentine officials as far back as 1944, and GUYDANO further reports that if Hitler is apprehended the names of these six top officials will be revealed.

"GUYDANO is ready also to reveal the names of the three other men who, with GUYDANO, helped Hitler inland to his hiding place.

"GUYDANO advised that he was given $15,000 for helping in the deal... realizing that it is only a matter of time before Hitler is apprehended, he is desirous of clearing himself at this time." — FBI Document dated August 14, 1945 (FBI Case File 65-53615. P.1. and P.2.).

The FBI headquarters file on Adolf Hitler, File 65-53615, began being released by the FBI to researchers under the Freedom of Information Act on 26 April 1976, though in a redacted form.

The first document 65-53615-35, which is heavily redacted in the version on the FBI website was completely opened to researchers by the FBI in 1991 and has been opened to researchers at the National Archives for over a dozen years.

Official sources: Zero evidence that Hitler died in Berlin
One investigator noted that:

- "American Army officials in Germany have not located Hitler's body nor is there any reliable source that Hitler is dead."

- DNA Tests on "Hitler's skull": Neither Hitler's nor Eva Brown's

But perhaps the most damning piece of evidence lies in Russia. With the Soviet occupation of Germany, Hitler's supposed remains were quickly hidden and sent off to Russia, never to be seen again.

That is until 2009, when an archaeologist from Connecticut State, Nicholas Bellantoni was allowed to perform DNA testing on one of the skull fragments recovered.

FBI Report (dated 14th July 1945) of Nazi submarines landing in Argentina.

What he sent offset off a reaction through the intelligence and scholarly communities. Not only did the DNA not match any recorded samples thought to be Hitler's, but Eva Braun's familiar DNA did not match either. "The bone seemed very thin; male bone tends to be more robust. And the sutures where the skull plates came together seemed to correspond to someone under 40."

Bellantoni's suspicions from the physical examination were confirmed authentic when they were backed up by molecular, genetic analysis.

The skull, which the Soviets had proffered as proof of Hitler's self-inflicted gunshot for decades, belonged to an unidentified female.

Whether or not you make a habit of doubting official stories, you should be able to see that despite the story we have been spoon-fed all these years, there is credible evidence to prove the contrary.

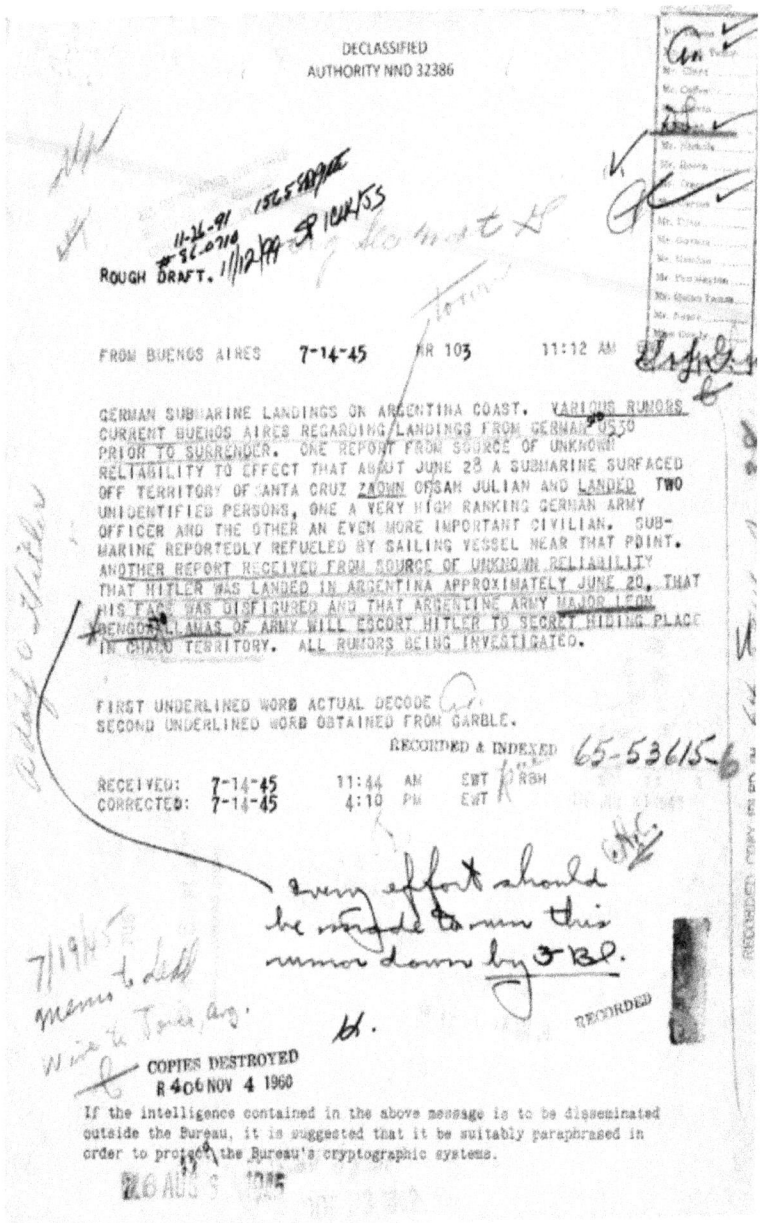

CHAPTER NINE

Hitler's Secret Argentine Sanctuary?

The house where Hitler spent the last years of his life, is reported to be a remote mansion similar to the infamous Berghof located in the Nahuel Huapi Lake, in Patagonia, Argentina, a remote mountainous paradise full of ashke Nazi refugees.

The mansion, called 'Residencia Inalco' was reported to be for sale after going through a few owners starting with Enrique García Merou, a Buenos Aires lawyer linked to several German-owned companies that allegedly collaborated in the escape to Argentina of high Nazi party members and SS officials. He bought the lot from architect Alejandro Bustillo, who created the original plans of the house in March 1943.

Bustillo also built other houses for Nazi fugitives who were later apprehended in the area. The terrain in which the house was erected, on Bajia Istana near the little town of Villa La Angostura, was quite remote and hardly accessible at the time.

The plans are similar to the architecture of Hitler's refuge in the Alps, with bedrooms connected by bathrooms and walk-in closets and a tea house located by a small farm.

Like Berghof, the Inalco house could only have been observed from the lake -a forest on the back limited the view from land. It even had Swiss cows imported by Merou from Europe.

Later, Merou sold the house to Jorge Antonio, who was connected to President Perón and was the German representative of Mercedes Benz in the South American country.

According to the book *'Grey Wolf: The Escape of Adolf Hitler'*, Hitler was already dead -after leaving behind two daughters -by the time the house was sold to José Rafael Trozzo in 1970.

Strangely enough, Trozzo also bought other properties owned by someone called Juan Mahler. Mahler was the fake name of Reinhard Kopps, SS official, and war criminal.

Kopps was connected to Erich Priebke, former Hauptsturmführer in the Waffen SS who participated in the massacre of the Ardeatine caves in Rome, in which 335 Italian civilians were executed after a partisan attack against SS forces.

Priebke was a respected member of the high society in the area. He was the director of a school Primo Capraro. The son of Capraro sold the Inalco house terrains to Bustillo.

The Trozzo family was reported to be selling the house and the original plans were been published, along with the Hitler legend recently resuscitated by *'Grey Wolf',* perhaps in an effort to increase the interest in the property.

The complex was completely autonomous, with its own animals and agricultural areas. It also had a ramp that led into the lake, with a boathouse that was rumored to contain a hydroplane.

An article by Claire Bernish in *The Event Chronicle* reads:

Long considered the purely fictitious musings of conspiracy theorists, rumors Adolf Hitler did not die in a murder-suicide pact with his newlywed, Eva Braun -but instead escaped to live under the radar in South America -might actually hold weight, after all.

Officially, whatever worth that could offer, Hitler met his fate with a gunshot to the head, while Braun ingested cyanide in a subterranean bunker on April 30, 1945, as the Allies finally quashed the Nazis. Forces then burned their bodies, and the pair were subsequently buried in a shallow grave nearby.

But what if this narrative had merely been a comfortable cover spoon-fed the public to mask the Führer actually being whisked away in a shadowy plot to ensure he wouldn't fall into the clutches of advancing Soviets?

If the thought perhaps seems a bit 'tin-foil for your taste, first consider the United States' morals-thwarting Operation Paperclip.

Nearly 500 Nazi scientists -particularly those specializing in aerodynamics, rocketry, chemical weapons and reaction technology, and medicine -were secreted to White Sands Proving Ground in New Mexico; Huntsville, Alabama; and Texas' Fort Bliss without even the knowledge of the State Department. As obvious security threats and war criminals, those scientists wouldn't have qualified for visas through official channels -but the government, foregoing ethical implications in pursuit of their knowledge, indeed facilitated safe passage to the U.S.

Though much information about what has alternately been called Project Paperclip remains classified, that Nazi scientists did receive paychecks courtesy of the U.S. government to advance national goals is admitted fact. In that context, would Hitler being given a similar VIP escape plan be that outside the realm of possibility?

Historian Abel Basti extensively details this hypothesis in a new edition of his book published in Argentina, '*El Exilio de Hitler*,' or '*Hitler in Exile*' -an account now making headlines, even in media as mainstream as the Huffington Post.

"There was an agreement with the US that Hitler would run away and that he shouldn't fall into the hands of the Soviet Union," Basti said. "This also applies to many scientists, the military and spies who later took part in the struggle against the Soviet regime."

Basti posits Hitler slipped to safety via a tunnel beneath the Chancellery connected to Tempelhof Airport, where a helicopter then whisked the former Führer to Spain. Traveling first to the Canary Islands, Hitler made his way to Argentina on a U-boat, where he lived for ten years before settling in Paraguay under the protection of dictator Alfredo Stroessner, himself with German roots.

As the historian tells it, the former brutal fascist died there on February 3, 1971. "Wealthy families who helped him over the years were responsible for the organization of his funeral," Basti explained. "Hitler was buried in an underground bunker, which is now an elegant hotel in the city of Asuncion. In 1973, the entrance to the bunker was sealed, and 40 people came to say goodbye to Hitler. One of those who attended [the funeral], Brazilian serviceman Fernando Nogueira de Araujo, then told a newspaper about the ceremony."

But Basti isn't alone in this hypothesis. Bob Baer, an experienced CIA operative and "one of America's most elite intelligence case officers, described a similarly covert, government-facilitated escape plan in a documentary series for the History Channel called Hunting Hitler, which aired in early 2015. Baer and his team, including war crimes investigator Dr. John Cencich, claimed they discovered proof of Hitler's escape, using 700 pages of declassified FBI documents and on-scene sleuthing in South America. As one investigator noted,

"American Army officials in Germany have not located Hitler's body nor is there any reliable source that Hitler is dead."

Further discrediting the official story -and backing up doubts raised by Basti and the Baer team -a report in the Guardian in 2009 shattered previously-'irrefutable' physical evidence of Hitler's suicide: the former Führer's bullet-pierced skull.

American researchers performed a DNA analysis of that skull once preserved in secret by Soviet intelligence, now held by Russian State Archive in Moscow -to determine the legitimacy of claims the bones were indeed Hitler's.

But in the genetics lab at the University of Connecticut, archeologist and bone specialist Nick Bellantoni made a startling discovery. From the outset, Bellantoni noticed telling discrepancies:

"The bone seemed very thin; male bone tends to be more robust. And the sutures where the skull plates came together seemed to correspond to someone under 40" -but Hitler turned 56 in April 1945. Bellantoni's suspicions from physical examination of that skull fragment -which the team diligently confirmed authentic -were backed up by the molecular, genetic analysis. That skull, which the Soviets had proffered as proof of Hitler's self-inflicted gunshot for decades, belonged to an as-yet-unidentified female.

Though possible the skull fragment, found to be of a "woman between the ages of 20 and 40," according to Bellantoni, could belong to Eva Braun, no narrative of events ever claimed Hitler's former bride was shot. And though many died near the Chancellery, the Soviets and then Russians verified the area from which the fragment was retrieved as the exact spot the couple's bodies had been doused in fuel and burned.

Further, Basti claims Braun not only also fled Germany unscathed, but far outlived Hitler -though he hasn't been able to track her past the age of 90, where she last resided in Buenos Aires. As early as 2000, the BBC reported Hitler biographer Werner Maser cast doubt on the authenticity of the skull -despite steadfast public affirmation from Russian officials.

South America did indeed play host to many fleeing Nazis -including sadistic doctor Josef Mengele, whose torturous experimentation of Nazi concentration camp prisoners eventually branched into the study of twins. Later, in a small town in Brazil, one in five pregnancies resulted in births of twins -something Argentine historian Jorge Camarasa claimed in 2009 evidenced Mengele's handiwork following his escape from Germany.

Whether or not you make a habit of doubting official stories, evidence of Hitler's deft departure from Germany -rather than a death by his own hand alongside his bride of just a few hours - appears more solid by the year.

As biographers, researchers, scientists, historians, and others carefully piece together a credible counter-narrative, perhaps Hitler's suicide stands as one more falsely constructed story designed to comfort an atrocity-weary public -as well as a veil the ethical avulsion of an awkward truth.

Mr. Cencich said: "The accepted truth that he committed suicide is ambiguous." When the war came to an end many Nazis made an exodus to South America to begin a new life away from Europe. It is claimed Hitler traveled by U-Boat to Argentina from the Canary Islands to be reunited with his comrades.

An article by Jesus Diaz reads: The Conspiracy Theorists might say, this was the house where Hitler spent the last years of his life, a remote mansion similar to the infamous Berghof located in the Nahuel Huapi Lake, in Patagonia, Argentina, a remote mountainous paradise full of Nazi refugees. The mansion -called residencia Inalco -was for sale after going through a few owners starting with Enrique García Merou, a Buenos Aires lawyer linked to several German-owned companies that allegedly collaborated in the escape to Argentina of high Nazi party members and SS officials.

He bought the lot from architect Alejandro Bustillo, who created the original plans of the house in March 1943. Bustillo also built other houses for Nazi fugitives who were later apprehended in the area. The terrain in which the house was erected, on Bajia Istana near the little town of Villa La Angostura, was quite remote and hardly accessible at the time.

The plans are similar to the architecture of Hitler's refuge in the Alps, with bedrooms connected by bathrooms and walk-in closets and a tea house located by a small farm.

Like Berghof, the Inalco house could only have been observed from the lake -a forest on the back limited the view from land. It even had Swiss cows imported by Merou from Europe.

Later, Merou sold the house to Jorge Antonio, who was connected to President Perón and was the German representative of Mercedes Benz in the South American country.

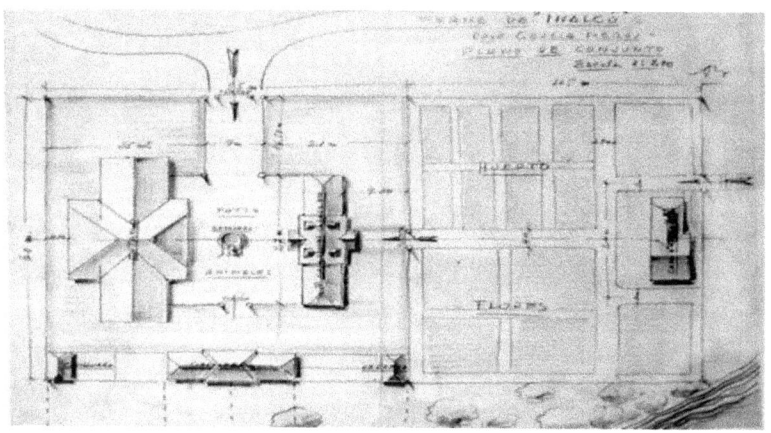

According to the book *'Grey Wolf: The Escape of Adolf Hitler'*, Hitler was already dead -after leaving behind two daughters -by the time the house was sold to José Rafael Trozzo in 1970. Strangely enough, Trozzo also bought other properties owned by someone called Juan Mahler. Mahler was the fake name of Reinhard Kopps, SS official, and war criminal.

The Berghof, Hitler's mansion in the Alps. Kopps was connected to Erich Priebke, former Hauptsturmführer in the Waffen SS who participated in the massacre of the Ardeatine caves in Rome, in which 335 Italian civilians were executed after a partisan attack against SS forces. Priebke was a respected member of the high society in the area. He was the director of a school Primo Capraro. The son of Capraro sold the Inalco house terrains to Bustillo.

The Trozzo family was intending to sell the house and the original plans were been published, along with the Hitler legend resuscitated by *Grey Wolf*, perhaps in an effort to increase the interest in the property.

The complex was completely autonomous, with its own animals and agricultural areas. It also had a ramp that led into the lake, with a boathouse that was rumored to contain a hydroplane.

CHAPTER TEN

THE CIA: HE'S ALIVE

In 1955, the Agency's South American station chief received what was purported to be photographic evidence Hitler was alive and well in Argentina. Written by JPat Brown and edited by Michael Morisy:

In 1955, the Central Intelligence Agency's chief of Western Hemisphere Division received a SECRET memo whose subject line no doubt caused them to sit up in their chair: "Operational: Adolf Hitler."

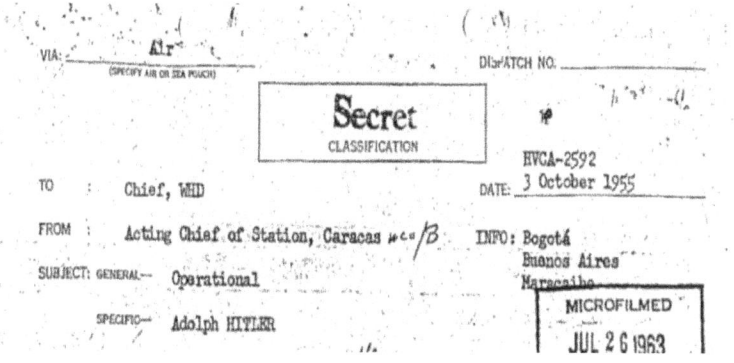

In the memo, the acting station chief in Venezuela claimed to have received an extraordinary tip from one of his contacts: *Hitler was alive! And living in Argentina!*

3. CIMELODY-3's friend stated that during the latter part of September 1955, a Phillip CITROEN, former German SS trooper, stated to him confidentially that Adolph HITLER is still alive. CITROEN claimed to have contacted HITLER about once a month in Colombia on his trip from Maracaibo to that country as an employee of the KNSM (Royal Dutch) Shipping Co. in Maracaibo. CITROEN indicated to CIMELODY-3's friend that he took a picture with HITLER not too long ago, but did not show the photograph. He also stated that HITLER left Colombia for Argentina around January 1955. CITROEN commented that inasmuch as ten years have passed since the end of World War II, the Allies could no longer prosecute HITLER as a criminal of war.

(Also, war crimes have a surprisingly tight statute of limitations.) Included in the memo was what purported to be photographic proof of the claim ...

Phillip Citroen (left), a former SS soldier, went to CIA agents in 1954 to say that he had seen a man claiming to be Adolf Hitler (right) alive and living in Colombia. Citroen gave agents this photo to support his claims.

As the memo helpfully points out, Hitler's supposed to be the one on the right -though if you really needed another clue, apparently, he was going by the pseudonym "Adolph Schuttlemayer."

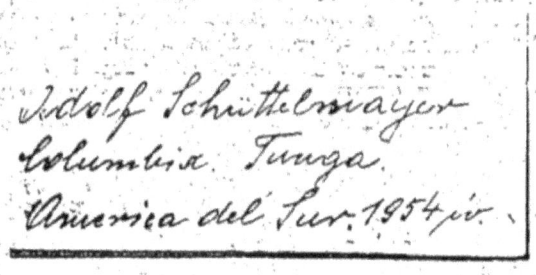

Way to keep a low profile there, Hitler.

The WHD chief followed up on the memo by reviewing the Agency's files, and sure enough, the year before there was a report from the contact's source, which not only made the same claim regarding Hitler not being dead but also that there was a whole colony of Nazis in South America, hanging out and saluting each other.

1. With reference to the information submitted by Station Caracas concerning the alleged report that Adolf HITLER is still alive, the files of the Base contain similar information received from the same source, who resides in Maracaibo.

2. An undated memorandum, believed to have been written in about mid February 1954, reflects that Phillip CITROEN, who was co-owner of the former Maracaibo Times, told a former member of this Base that while he was working for a railroad company in Colombia, he had met an individual who strongly resembled and claimed to be Adolf HITLER. CITROEN claimed to have met this individual at a place called "Residencias Coloniales" in Tunja, (Boyaca), Colombia, which is, according to the source, overly populated with former German Nazis. According to CITROEN, the Germans residing in Tunja follow this alleged Adolf HITLER with an "idolatry of the Nazi past, addressing him as 'der Fuhrer' and affording him the Nazi salute and storm-trooper adulation".

Again, Simpsons did it.

A few days later, the understandably agitated station chief wrote the WHD chief again, asking if they wanted to do anything about this Hitler thing or not.

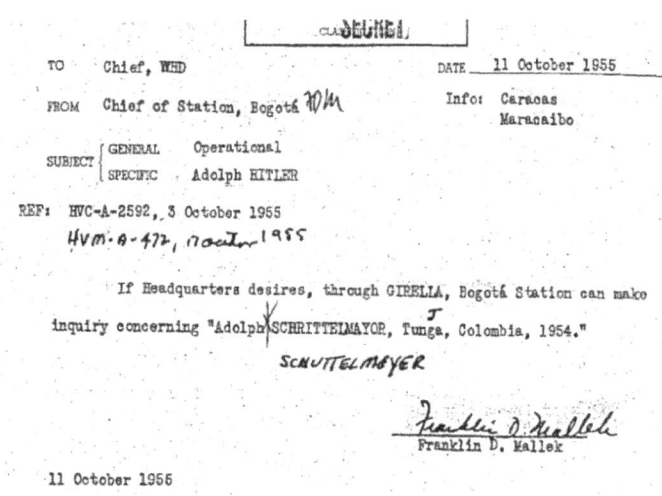

Seeing as it was shaping up to be a whole lot of work just for something as minor as determining if Hitler was still alive or not, the WHD recommended the whole thing just be dropped.

And dropped it was. As for Hitler, depending on who you ask, he either continued to be dead, or he is doing just fine at 128.

CHAPTER ELEVEN

Hitler in Colombia?

The year was 1955, the source a CIA informant, the claim explosive. Amongst the recently declassified CIA documents on the JFK assassination was an incredible revelation that no one expected. Buried in the documents was a report that claimed Hitler survived the Second World War and was living in Colombia. The informant, codenamed 'Cimelody-3', told the acting US intelligence chief for Venezuela that he was in contact with a former SS agent, Philip Citroen, who met a man claiming to be Adolf Hitler in Tunja, Colombia.

The supervisor took the information seriously. So seriously, in fact, that he passed it on the CIA directly, "Cimelody-3 was contacted on 29 September 1955 by a trusted friend who served under his command in Europe and who is presently residing in Maracaibo," the Intelligence chief wrote. "Cimelody-3 friend stated that during the latter part of September 1955, Phillip Citroen, former German SS trooper, stated to him confidentially that Adolph Hitler is still alive."

The document reports that Citroen met the man claiming to be Hitler, referred to as Adolf Schuttlemayer, at a place called Residencies Coloniales, Colombia. The memo details that "According to Citroen, the Germans residing in Tunja follow this alleged Adolf Hitler with an idolatry of the Nazi past, addressing him as Elder Fuhrer and affording him the Nazi salute and storm-trooper adulation."

Along with the memo, there was a photo, a grainy image of Citroen with Schuttlemayer who clearly resembles the former Nazi leader.

Allegedly, by the time the CIA took the claim seriously, it was too late, Schuttlemayer had fled to Argentina. Was this just a crazed fame seeker or does this story have depth?

One thing we can say for certain is that ex-CIA agent Bob Baer will be listening. For the last few years, Baer has been leading a team of investigators on a manhunt that asks the question, did Hitler survive the Second World War?

Hunting Hitler has seen Baer and his team travel across South America on the mission to find evidence that supports the claim the Nazi leader escaped there after WW II. While there have been clues that point to the above this new claim is sure to add intrigue to the series. It's believed that thousands of Nazis fled to South America after WW II, could Hitler have been amongst them? Speaking to Baer earlier this year he told HISTORY, "What I like doing is going through the files as they are declassified and finding out what's missed. Remember, in most criminal cases the full extent of them is never known until years later."

The stage is set for the next chapter in Baer's investigation. The ex-CIA agent and his team will undoubtedly be working overtime as they pore through this new evidence. This is yet another fascinating fallout from the recently declassified CIA files on JFK, and as the story develops it begs the question, what other secrets do they contain?

VIA:	Air		DISPATCH NO.	
		Secret	HVCA-2592	
		CLASSIFICATION		
TO	: Chief, WHD		DATE: 3 October 1955	
FROM	: Acting Chief of Station, Caracas		INFO: Bogotá	
			Buenos Aires	
SUBJECT: GENERAL—	Operational		Maracaibo	
SPECIFIC—	Adolph HITLER		MICROFILMED JUL 26 1963	

fairly reliable

1. On 29 September 1955, CIMELODY-3 reported the following. Neither CIMELODY-3 nor this Station is in a position to give an intelligent evaluation of the information and it is being forwarded as of possible interest.

2. CIMELODY-3 was contacted on 29 September 1955 by a trusted friend who served under his command in Europe and who is presently residing in Maracaibo. CIMELODY-3 preferred not to reveal the identity of his friend.

3. CIMELODY-3's friend stated that during the latter part of September 1955, a Phillip CITROEN, former German SS trooper, stated to him confidentially that Adolph HITLER is still alive. CITROEN claimed to have contacted HITLER about once a month in Colombia on his trip from Maracaibo to that country as an employee of the KNSM (Royal Dutch) Shipping Co. in Maracaibo. CITROEN indicated to CIMELODY-3's friend that he took a picture with HITLER not too long ago, but did not show the photograph. He also stated that HITLER left Colombia for Argentina around January 1955. CITROEN commented that inasmuch as ten years have passed since the end of World War II, the Allies could no longer prosecute HITLER as a criminal of war.

4. On 28 September 1955, CIMELODY-3's friend surreptitiously obtained the photograph which CITROEN referred to. On 29 September 1955, the photo was shown to CIMELODY-3 for purposes of getting his reaction to the possible veracity of this fantastic story. Obviously, CIMELODY-3 was not in any position to make any comments. Nonetheless, he borrowed the photograph long enough so that this Station could take any action deemed advisable. Photostats of this picture were taken, and are being forwarded. The photograph was to be returned to its owner the following day. The person on the left is alleged to be CITROEN and the person on the right is undoubtedly the person which CITROEN claims is HITLER. The back side of the photograph contained the following data: "Adolf SCHRITTELMAYOR, Tunga, Colombia, 1954."

DNB/lac

Attachment: 1 photo

David N. Brixnor

3 October 1955
- Headquarters, w/1 att. in dupl.
- Bogotá, w/1 att., 1 copy
- Buenos Aires, w/1 att., 1 copy
- Maracaibo, w/1 att., 1 copy
- Files, w/1 att., 1 copy

Citroen said 'Hitler' was living in a community of ex-Nazis in the town of Tunja, near Bogota, under the name Adolf Schuttlemayer (pictured is the CIA file with the image attached).

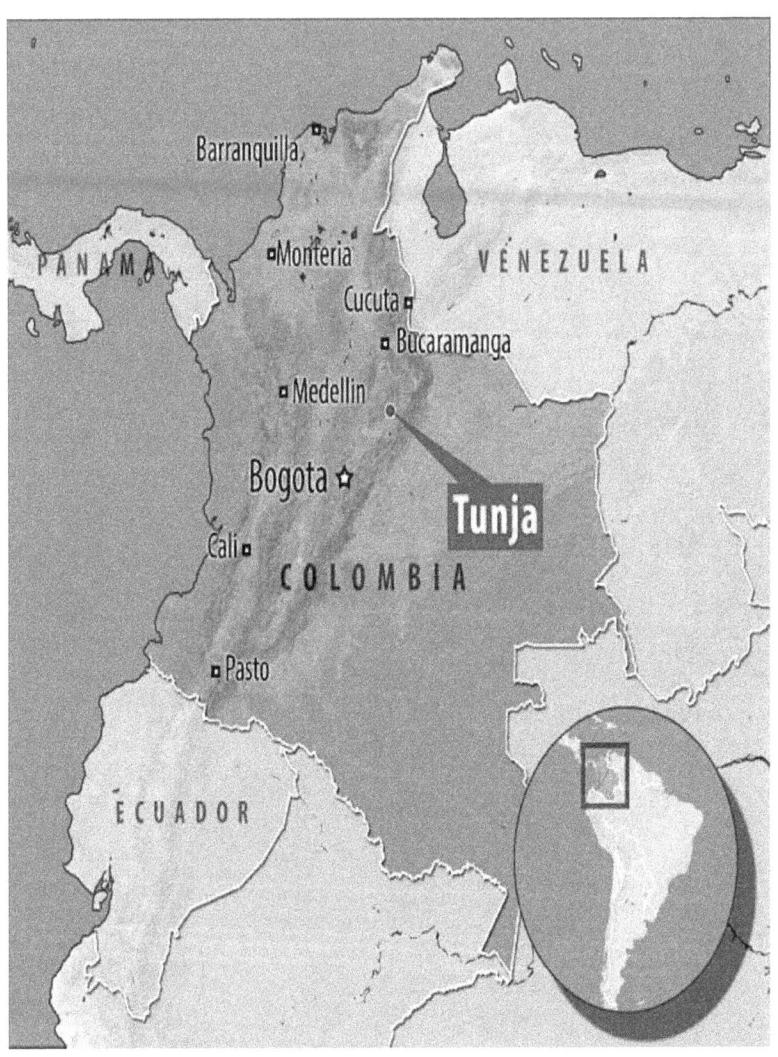

Thousands of Nazis fled Europe for South America after the Third Reich collapsed, mostly to Argentina, though some were found living in Colombia. Pictured is the town of Tunja, where the man claiming to be Hitler was living.

Citroen said the former Nazis called the man The Fuhrer, offered him Nazi salutes, and 'afforded him storm-trooper adulation'.

CHAPTER TWELVE

CIA Veteran Claims: Hitler 'Faked His Own Death

The bombshell revelations are made by Bob Baer -who claims he has 'proof' the Nazi leader survived the Second World War -in the new TV series Hunting Hitler for The History Channel. Rhian Lubin, Specialist Journalist, and Stephen Jones, Senior Assistant Editor, reported in the Mirror on 15th January 2017.

A veteran CIA agent claims he has proof that Adolf Hitler 'faked his own death and then fled to South America in a submarine via Tenerife'. The Nazi leader is famously meant to have committed suicide alongside his wife Eva Braun in his bunker at the tail end of the Second World War.

But Bob Baer and his team have scoured never-before-seen documents which he says shows 'the evilest man in history' in fact survived the allied invasion of Berlin - and beyond.

Moreover, they claim Hitler made it all the way to Argentina -first by Luftwaffe plane and then via a submarine which collected him from the Canary Islands.

There, they claim, he intended to lead the 'Fourth Reich' from a secure military compound. CIA veteran, Bob Baer is one of America's most elite intelligence case officers. Bob spent the majority of his career on the front edge of international espionage, counter-intelligence, and information gathering. From decoding and intercepting illicit weapons trades between countries to tracking some of the most elusive and high-profile terrorists, Bob has seen and done it all and is driven by the quest to know the truth regardless of the consequences. Bringing his expertise to this case, Bob will expertly sift through the thousands of recently declassified international documents to focus the field team on the most crucial and actionable intelligence.

He has led international teams of intelligence officers, informants, and officials across nations and through dangerous wartime situations, from the moment a message is intercepted through the process of bringing criminals to justice. He has long held reservations and doubts about the reports of Hitler's demise.

Bob Baer, assisted by US special forces sergeant Tim Kennedy, who was involved in the capture of Osama Bin Laden -explained: "The narrative the government gives us is a lie.

"If you look at the FBI files it throws open the investigation."

"What we are doing is re-examining history, a history that we thought was settled that Hitler died in the bunker but the deeper we get into it, it's clear to me we don't have any facts for it." Mr. Baer's team claims to have access to 700 pages of declassified information. One document, purportedly from British Intelligence, is said to claim Hitler was secretly flown out of the German capital by Luftwaffe pilot Captain Peter Baumgart.

Another document states: "American Army officials in Germany have not located Hitler's body nor is there any reliable source that Hitler is dead."

The team claim Hitler 'easily' faked his own death through the use of a double, as the corpse found by Russians was said to be five inches shorter than Hitler and with a smaller skull.

The duo also claims to have found evidence of a fifth exit from the bunker -which has never previously been reported.

Conspiracy: The team believe German dictator Adolf Hitler faked his own death (Image: Getty Images)

Ex-United Nations war crimes investigator John Cencich also interviews an alleged witness to Hitler's escape for the TV series.

The Greek former construction worker tells Mr. Cencich: "In 1945, I was building a secret construction inside the monastery in Samos."

"I had to build secret tunnels and compartments for Germans," he continued. "Yes, the Germans were Nazis and one of these guys was Adolf Hitler.

"He was right there; he wasn't wearing a moustache or anything. this was May 1945.

"I realised it was really Hitler because of the airplane.

"I went to work in another town. The first thing I saw in this town was a German airplane. It had landed in an old potato field. The farmer told me there were five people who landed, they were German."

CHAPTER THIRTEEN

THE REAL STORY OF HITLER'S DEATH?

Reed Tucker reported in the New York Post on 4th September 2018 that in August 1946, a Maryland man went to his usual lunch spot for a bite to eat. Finding the diner full, he asked a man sitting alone if he could share his table. The man, as it supposedly turned out, was Adolf Hitler.

The dictator was dressed "cheaply" and "very nervous," according to the witness. Hitler fidgeted and played with his napkin. His lunchmate called the authorities.

In 1948, a letter arrived at a Spanish-language newspaper. The writer claimed he'd last seen Hitler in Bogota, Colombia, 10 days previously and that he was "in perfect health." The Fuehrer had plans to conquer the moon and Mars.

Conspiracy theories regarding the death of Hitler are legion. Tales about his escape from a German bunker began cropping up just a few hours after his supposed death on April 30, 1945.

In 2018, a new book claimed to put the kibosh on all the rumors and definitively solved the mystery of what happened to the Nazi monster.

"The Death of Hitler: The Final Word" (Da Capo Press) is written by French journalist Jean-Christophe Brisard and Russian documentary maker Lana Parshina.

The duo ventured to Moscow to comb historical documents stored in secret archives. They were also allowed to examine a skull fragment containing a bullet hole and teeth supposedly taken from the German leader's body stored at the library belonging to Russia's notorious Federal Security Services.

The authors spent months negotiating for access to the depositories presided over by stern former-Soviet librarians and humorless guards wearing severe black uniforms. "How foreigners -even Lana with her perfect Russian and her old Russian passport- like us could get official access, that was the biggest challenge," Brisard tells The Post.

Among the 7 million documents stored in the Russian archives, the authors found top-secret accounts detailing the interrogations of members of Hitler's inner circle, who were captured when Soviet troops took Berlin.

What emerged was a detailed, if sometimes frustratingly contradictory, chronicle of Hitler's final days.

By April 1945, the Fuehrer had retreated to a heavily fortified underground bunker near the Reich Chancellery at 77 Wilhelmstrasse. On April 29, with Russian troops just blocks away, Hitler married girlfriend Eva Braun in a 10-minute ceremony. Just before the union, Hitler dictated his will to his private secretary. The document stated that he and Braun had chosen death and that their bodies should be burned upon discovery.

Hitler tested cyanide on his dog, Blondi, preparing for the end.

The next afternoon, he emerged from his room and quietly said goodbye to his closest aides. What happened next is unclear.

Hitler's valet, Heinz Linge, was stationed outside the door and told the Russians he heard a gunshot. He ran to alert Hitler's secretary Martin Bormann, and the two entered the room to find their leader and his wife dead.

The bodies were wrapped in blankets, carried upstairs, doused with gasoline, and burned. These teeth were analyzed to determine if they belonged to Adolf Hitler.

Death of Hitler:

The Russian files reveal that the Soviets collected numerous accounts (often under extreme duress) of the events from other bunker dwellers, and the interrogators grew irritated by the disparities, believing they were being lied to.

Some Nazis reported hearing a shot, others didn't. Some reported seeing a bullet wound in Hitler's head, others didn't. Had Hitler shot himself in the mouth of the temple? Or had he not shot himself at all and instead taken cyanide?

The Soviets preferred the latter narrative because they believed it showed cowardice on Hitler's part. A 1945 Russian autopsy performed on the burned corpses recovered near the entrance to the bunker backed up the cyanide hypothesis. A crushed glass capsule was found in the man's mouth and the smell of bitter almond was strong, indicating the poison.

The bodies were then buried, although they were later exhumed and cremated. But fragments of the jawbone were saved.

Indiana Jones of graveyards" for his role in identifying high-profile historical bodies.

Charlier was acceptable to the Russians, not just because of his reputation, but because he was not American. Anything but an American.

The skull piece was discovered by the Soviets in 1946, near where the burned bodies were found. It was stored in an archival safe, uncataloged until stumbled upon by a librarian in 1975.

To examine this physical evidence, the authors brought in Philippe Charlier, a French forensic pathologist.

The cautious Russians allowed only a visual analysis of the skull piece, and Charlier was able to determine that it belonged to an adult male and that it had been burned. But was it, Hitler's? The doctor couldn't say.

Hitler's teeth provided more clarity. Charlier was able to compare the jawbone with X-rays taken of Hitler in 1944. His conclusion? It was a match. No doubt. There was "perfect agreement."

Hitler did not escape Berlin in 1945. He died in that bunker. But the how of Hitler's demise remained a mystery.

Charlier was also allowed to analyze the teeth with a microscope and discovered strange blue stains. Charlier was stumped. Could cyanide have caused the discoloration?

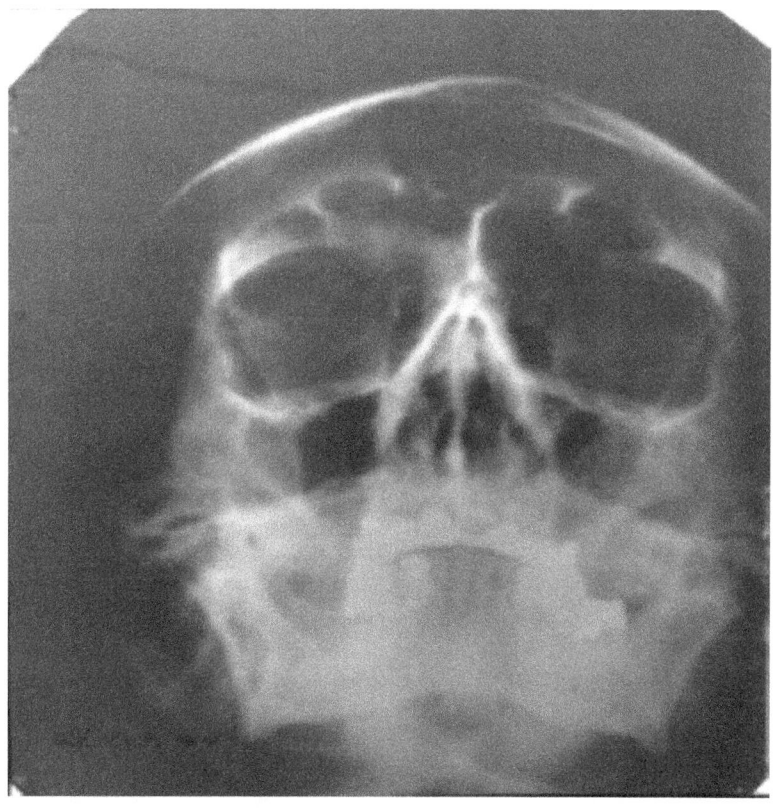

[A 1944 skull X-ray of Hitler. An expert was able to match teeth to those in the X-ray]

One of the bigger breakthroughs came completely by accident. Once Charlier had returned to France after the initial examination, he discovered some nearly microscopic pieces of dental tartar from Hitler's teeth stuck to the rubber gloves he wore for the examination.

He examined these grains by electron microscope and found more evidence strengthening the case. Within the sample, he discovered vegetable fibers but no meat, indicating the teeth belonged to a vegetarian, as Hitler was.

The tartar also was scanned for traces of three metallic elements that would indicate that Hitler had shot himself in the mouth, as his chauffeur, Erich Kempka, had told the British in 1945.

No traces were found, meaning Hitler almost certainly shot himself in the temple, as some witnesses stated.

As for the cyanide? Charlier was unable to come to any conclusion and is still unsure what caused the blue stains on the teeth. Without a more thorough examination, they will remain a mystery.

And Russia apparently isn't exactly welcoming any new inquiries. The teeth -among the most fascinating historical artifacts of the 20th century -were returned to the repurposed cigarillo box in which they've been casually stored, wheeled deep into the archives, and dropped onto a shelf alongside God knows what other relics. It is unclear when, or if, they will ever be seen again.

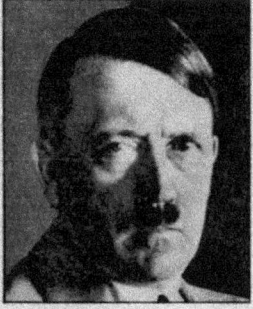

WANTED- DEAD OR ALIVE poster for Hitler appeared on the front page of the Daily Mirror on 4 September 1939 [Coursey: British Library Newspaper Archive. Image Copyright: John Frost Newspapers]

BERLIN FALLS! HITLER ALIVE! poster on the front page of the Stop Express.

HITLER IS ALIVE poster appeared on the front page of Weekly World News

CHAPTER FOURTEEN

'HITLER LIVED'

Delving into UK and US intel files, a British historian takes aim at the myriad of nonsensical stories that Hitler managed to escape and live out his life in peace.

Robert Philpot, London, reported in The Times of Israel on 2nd May 2019:

In November 1945, the British Legation in Copenhagen informed the Foreign Office that a Danish lady had reported to it her friend's dream that Adolf Hitler was alive, disguised as a monk, and had shaved off his mustache.

In London, civil servants understandably scoffed at the report and noted that "there will be no end to stories of this kind."

As British academic Luke Daly-Groves writes in his new book, "*Hitler's Death*" -a work that aims to rebut conspiracy theories surrounding the Führer's demise -those words have proved somewhat prophetic.

In the weeks and months after the war, Hitler sightings from across the world were reported to British and American intelligence services.

Hitler, it was claimed, had been seen in Ireland dressed as a woman; in Egypt where he had converted to Islam; in a coffee house in Amsterdam; on a train traveling from New Orleans; in a Washington, DC, restaurant; and in Charlottesville, Virginia.

And, most famously, there were multiple reports that Hitler was living with old comrades in Argentina, having, by some accounts, been spirited out of Berlin, flown to a German airbase in Denmark, and then taken across the Atlantic by u-boat. The Führer, one FBI file reported, had arrived at his Argentinian ranch hideaway by horseback.

Image by Bundesarchiv Bild shows Adolf Hitler and his mistress Eva Braun posing on the terrace of the Berghof, Berchtesgaden, in Germany in June 1942 (Courtesy: 'Hitler's Death' by Luke Daly-Groves).

"Hitler at this stage could undoubtedly have written one of the most comprehensive travel guides of the 20th century," Daly-Groves wryly argues. "But, of course, all available evidence suggests that such rumors were nonsense."

However nonsensical, so many years after he shot himself in Berlin and brought to a close the darkest chapter in human history, these rumors continue to feed a lucrative industry of Hitler conspiracy theories.

In later years, books such as *'Grey Wolf: The Escape of Adolf Hitler'* by Simon Dunstan and Gerrard Williams; Harry Cooper's

'*Hitler in Argentina: The Documented Truth of Hitler's Escape from Berlin*', have all pushed the notion that Hitler did not die as the Soviets advanced on Berlin, but lived out his final years in South America.

The books have been boosted by extensive newspaper coverage and supplemented by TV shows such as the History Channel's multi-part series, '*Hunting Hitler*.'

This latest wave of conspiracy-mongering was sparked by the revelation in 2009 that DNA tests had shown that a piece of skull in Moscow which was believed to have been Hitler's actually belonged to a woman.

CHAPTER FIFTEEN

Soviet Fake News

It was Soviet behavior immediately after Nazi Germany's defeat that provided the initial grist for the seemingly never-ending rumor mill. While Soviet officers working for Marshal Zhukov, who commanded the Russian forces in the Battle of Berlin, initially told Western newspapers that Hitler's body had been found, Stalin soon contradicted them. Less than a month after the war's end, the Soviet leader told former president Franklin D. Roosevelt's close confidant, Harry Hopkins, that Hitler was still alive. Within days, Zhukov had reversed course and said that the Führer's body had not been found and that he may indeed have escaped.

The Soviets' claims soon gained ground in Berlin and began to be reported in Allied newspapers. Thus, in July 1945, British newspapers reported comments by a Russian officer that a charred body discovered by the Soviets was "a very poor double." Across the Atlantic, US newspapers ran quotes attributed to the Russian garrison commandant of Berlin that Hitler had "gone into hiding somewhere in Europe," with the Spanish dictator, General Francisco Franco, fingered for potentially sheltering him.

The concerted and officially backed nature of the Soviet campaign was evident in the fact that, in September 1945, all Russian newspapers ran an item asserting that British intelligence officers were hunting for Hitler in Hamburg, with the Führer's appearance reportedly altered by a "plastic operation."

The Communist Party mouthpiece, Pravda, also ran comments by the deputy mayor of Berlin who was "convinced Hitler was alive." Such was the persistence of the Soviets' claims that, one month later, the Supreme Allied Commander, Dwight Eisenhower, suggested that Hitler might still be alive. The future president swiftly retracted the statement -which has nonetheless not prevented it from being widely repeated.

Daly-Groves believes that these Soviet actions have contributed to the endurance of conspiracy theories.

"One of the reasons these stories are still going strong is because, in a large part, they originate with the Soviet government, so they have important officials, such as Stalin, who took part in the defeat of Nazi Germany, saying that they believe Hitler could have escaped," Daly-Groves tells The Times of Israel.

Stalin's motives have been much speculated upon by historians. Some believe that the Soviet leader wanted to discredit popular potential rivals at home, such as Zhukov. Attempting to place the blame on Spain and Argentina for sheltering Hitler served to help undermine Stalin's fascist enemies overseas. He may also have wished to maintain the notion of a continuing threat from Hitler as part of a power play in territorial disputes as the Allies moved into their zones of occupation in Germany.

Indeed, some historians suggest that in this early example of fake news, there are parallels with Vladimir Putin. As the historian Guy Walters wrote: "Stalin was keen -just like his successor in the Kremlin today -to sow division and discord in the West by suggesting that the British or Americans were sheltering Hitler."

Daly-Groves doesn't dispute the possibility of any of these motives. However, he adds one of his own: that the Soviet leader may have been embarrassed by the bungled investigation into Hitler's death carried out by his forces when they took control of Berlin. The shoddy nature of this probe is exemplified by the fact that the first Soviets to enter the Führerbunker were a group of women who proceeded to steal Eva Braun's lingerie.

"That just sets the tone for the Soviet investigation," says Daly-Groves.

In the 2009, DNA test results thus may simply point to the fact that the Soviets' inquiries in the days after Hitler's death were more botched than previously thought. Perhaps, he speculates, soldiers ordered by Stalin to determine Hitler's whereabouts were too terrified to say they hadn't been able to recover his body and "picked up whatever mush they could find in front of Hitler's bunker exit, put it in a box and claimed it was the corpses of Adolf and Eva Hitler, when in reality all that was left was little more than teeth, ash and a garbled mess, barely recognizable as a 'body.'"

CHAPTER SIXTEEN

THE TREVOR-ROPER DOSSIER

The Russian disinformation campaign did not, however, go unchallenged, with Britain appointing the historian Hugh Trevor-Roper in September 1945 to conduct its own investigation into what occurred in the bunker in Hitler's last days. While the Soviets blocked access to forensic evidence (they did not finally release it for two decades), Trevor-Roper managed to compile a dossier of compelling eyewitness accounts that Hitler had taken his own life in the face of impending defeat, and that his body, along with that of Braun, was incinerated in the ruins of his Chancellery Garden as Russian shells rained down.

Because of this conclusion, which was later released in his best-selling book, Trevor-Roper has subsequently been heavily targeted by conspiracy theorists. Gerrard Williams, the co-author of "Grey Wolf," for instance, told British television in 2011: "I have no idea why Hugh Trevor-Roper was actually chosen by the Secret Services to do the death of Hitler."

Trevor-Roper is accused of being unqualified for the task and his work is alleged to have been driven by a political desire to clear Britain of Soviet insinuations of harboring Hitler. The fact that, in 1983, he also initially believed the infamous Hitler diaries – ultimately revealed to be the work of a German fraudster – to be genuine, has also been used to undermine the credibility of his investigation in 1945.

But, Daly-Groves argues, Trevor-Roper was eminently qualified to examine whether Hitler had escaped. A highly regarded MI6 officer who had taught himself, German, he was also renowned for having cracked an Abwehr code while soaking in the bath during an air raid. "You only have to read the biography of Trevor-Roper to see how skilled he was in intelligence and why he was chosen," he suggests. "He was the foremost expert on the German intelligence services at the time and if anybody was going to help Hitler escape it was going to be the German intelligence services because it would have involved a major covert operation."

Daly-Groves believes any errors Trevor-Roper made in 1983 as a then-elderly man should not reflect on his work in 1945. "His letters show how meticulous he was and that his motivations were to discover the truth about the past," Daly-Groves argues. "It's very clear to me that if he had any credible evidence to suggest that Hitler escaped, he would have been one of the first to go out to try and catch him."

Daly-Groves's examination of British intelligence files proves he claims, that conspiracy theorists' allegations about the UK's motivations for appointing Trevor-Roper are far off the mark. Britain was keen to scotch rumors that Hitler was hiding in their zone because it believed they threatened to sour the prospects of postwar cooperation with the Russians.

It was also concerned to prevent the growth of a "Hitler myth" – based on the notion that he was either alive or had died heroically – from developing. Such a myth, it was feared, might hinder de-Nazification in Germany and be also being used to encourage last-ditch Nazi resistance efforts and, later, neo-Nazi underground movements.

Finally, the British wanted the truth about Hitler's death recorded for posterity.

"The book is intended as history rather than propaganda," Trevor-Roper informed intelligence chiefs in London.

CHAPTER SEVENTEEN

The Flip side of Seeking Truth: 'Overwhelming and Comprehensive' Evidence

Daly-Groves concludes his book by asserting that it is "beyond all reasonable doubt" that Hitler committed suicide as Berlin went up in flames on April 30, 1945. What makes him so sure? The evidence, he maintains, is "overwhelming and comprehensive."

There are the words of Hitler himself, contained in his last will and testament, which explicitly stated that he and Braun had chosen to die in the capital of the Reich.

There are the late Führer's teeth and jaw, which now sit in a Moscow archive. They were first positively identified for the Russians by two of Hitler's dentists. Only last year, a team of forensic scientists compared the remains to records produced by his dentists. Again, the conclusion was clear: Despite some conspiracy theorists' maintaining that the body burned by the bunker was that of a double, the teeth in Moscow are those of Hitler.

But perhaps most compelling is the testimony from multiple eyewitnesses. One of the "most important" interrogations conducted for Trevor-Roper's report, suggests Daly-Groves, was that of Hermann Karnau, a guard on duty outside the bunker on the day of Hitler's death.

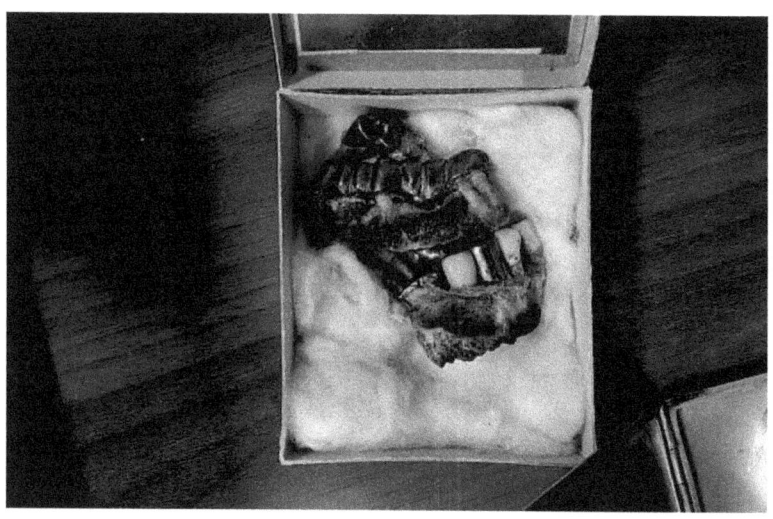

Adolf Hitler's teeth. (Russian State Archives)

Ordered away from the Chancellery for a time by the SS, he returned to see the burning bodies of Hitler and Braun "two meters from the emergency exit." A sketch he provided to investigators of the location where the couple were buried – which closely matches similar diagrams in Soviet documents -is published by Daly-Groves for the first time. Another guard interviewed by intelligence officers corroborated Karnau's testimony.

"What's so convincing about these eyewitness testimonies to me," Daly-Groves suggests, "is that many of them are circumstantial."

Aside from Karnau, for instance, there is a witness who overheard a phone call in which Hitler's bodyguard, Otto Günsche, ordered the Führer's chauffeur, Erich Kempka, to bring 200 liters (about 53 gallons) of petrol to the bunker.

"People who weren't supposed to see and hear things saw and heard things," argues Daly-Groves. "It all adds up."

The same cannot, perhaps, be said for the tales of Hitler roaming across Argentina on horseback, sipping coffee in Amsterdam, or riding the railroad through the American Deep South with which Britain and America's intelligence services had to contend in the days, weeks, and months after his death.

CHAPTER EIGHTEEN

The Skul, Jaws and Teeth

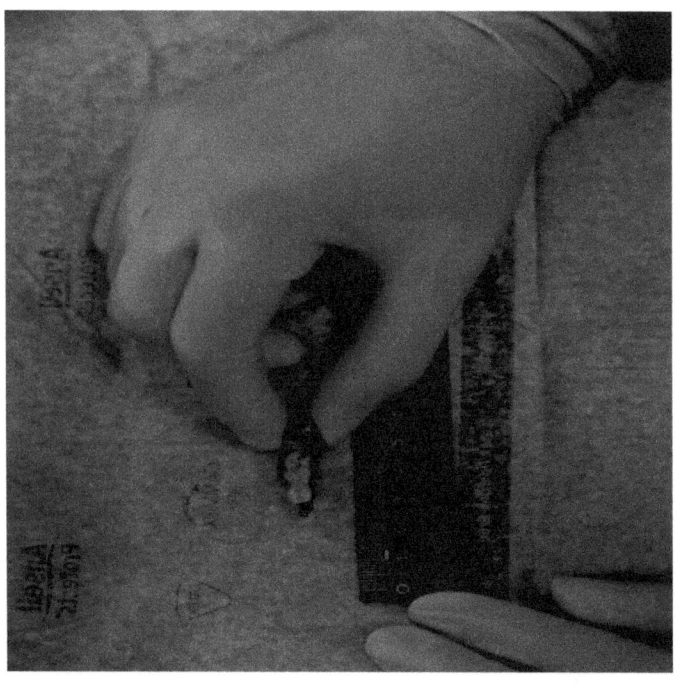

Philippe Charlier examined Hitler's teeth to find proof of how he died *(Twitter: Philippe Charlier)*.

French scientists are saying they have conclusively proved Hitler died in 1945. The majority of historians believe Hitler committed suicide in his Berlin bunker, and a study published on 18th May 2018 in the European Journal of Internal Medicine claims to present evidence the Nazi dictator died from taking cyanide and a bullet to the head.

The study examined Hitler's teeth, which were put on display in an exhibition in Moscow in 2000, and appears to back up the widely held view he died on April 30, 1945, with his companion Eva Braun.

The analysis found white tartar deposits and no traces of meat fibre, as Hitler was vegetarian.

It also revealed bluish deposits on his false teeth, an indication of the chemical reaction between cyanide and the metal of his dentures.

The team also looked at a skull fragment, said to be from the German dictator, which showed a hole on the left side in all probability caused by a bullet. Professor Philippe Charlier, who headed the study, said the teeth were undoubtedly Hitler's and proved he died at the end of World War II.

"We can stop all the conspiracy theories about Hitler. He did not flee to Argentina in a submarine, he is not in a hidden base in Antarctica or on the dark side of the moon," he said.

Historians believe Hitler took his own life as Russian forces closed in during the final stages of the battle for Berlin. It is believed his body was hastily cremated near his bunker, with the teeth and other fragmentary remains later seized by Russian officials and sent back to Moscow on the orders of Soviet dictator Josef Stalin.

With Germany's defeat imminent, Adolf Hitler and his wife Eva Braun committed suicide on April 30, 1945. Per his orders, the bodies were taken outside of the bunker, doused in 200 liters of benzene, and lit on fire. The remains were buried in a shallow grave until they were recovered by the Soviet secret service a few days later; they were burned again by the KBG in April 1970. This, however, is not the history some conspiracy theorists believe.

That's why scientists behind a new *European Journal of Internal Medicine* paper had to dig back into his remains to settle the truth.

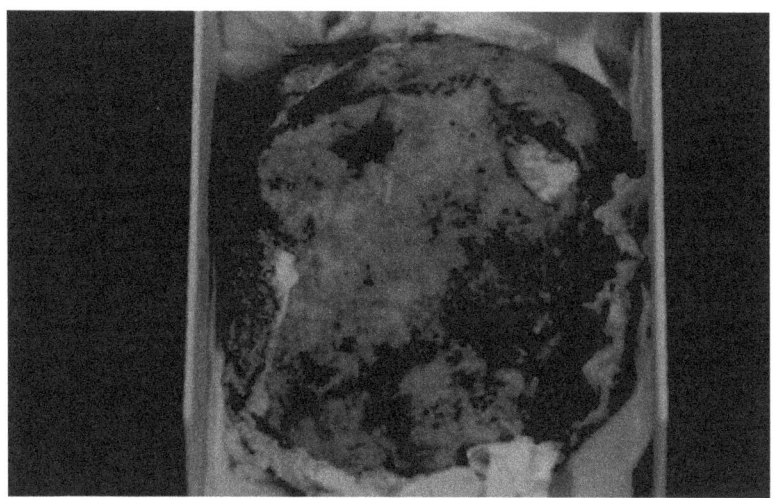

A piece of Hitler's skull demonstrates the projectile exit wound.
European Journal of Internal Medicine

This analysis, the study authors note in their paper, published Friday, lays to rest the multitude of conspiracy theories that claim Hitler did not die by suicide in a bunker. Some of these myths were spread by Soviet and German forces after the war. In the radio announcement of his death, his successor Karl Dönitz claimed Hitler died in battle. Joseph Stalin, who knew that an autopsy had confirmed that the remains belonged to Hitler and Braun, nurtured rumors that Hitler was alive and had fled. The FBI seriously investigated claims that Hitler was living in South America, while theories that Hitler was on the moon or in Antarctica continued to circulate.

But in the new paper, a biomedical analysis of the only two remaining fragments of Hitler -a part of his skull and his jaws, both in Russian possession -surfaces unshakeable evidence that Hitler committed suicide in Germany.

"Our study proves that Hitler died in 1945," study co-author Phillipe Charlier, Ph.D. told *Agence France-Presse*. "We can stop all the conspiracy theories about Hitler. He did not flee to Argentina in a submarine, he is not in a hidden base in Antarctica or on the dark side of the moon."

The Russian government allowed Charlier and his team to analyze the skull and teeth in March and July 2017, which the authors claim is the first time the remains have been examined since World War II. Writing that the study allows them to end a "scientific and historical fantasy," the scientists compare the remains to historical documents. That process, they write, provides support for the long-standing official account of Hitler's death: that he swallowed a cyanide pill then shot himself in the head.

Skull

While the scientists weren't permitted to take samples from the skull fragment, its morphology was comparable to the radiography data collected from Hitler's skull a year before his death. On the left side is a hole, which was determined to be caused by a bullet."Recent analysis of the biomedical literature related to cremation of human remains shows that fragmentation of the skull, lack of extremities, and surface alterations described on the supposed remains of Adolf Hitler are fully compatible with the historical testimonies of cremation, inhumation, and exhumation," the scientists write.

Jaws and Teeth

Hitler's dentist and dental technician had already confirmed, during a Soviet investigation in 1945, that the jaw and teeth belonged to Hitler. In addition, they matched reports that Hitler had only a few of his own teeth remaining at the time of his death and showed evidence of his "conspicuous and unusual prostheses and bridgework." The teeth also show no traces of meat, adding evidence to the claim that Hitler was a vegetarian.

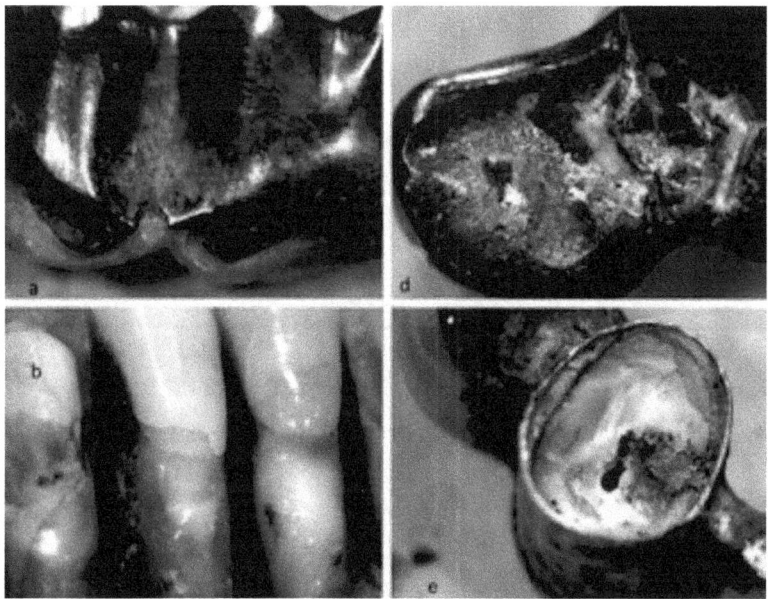

The skull/jaw remains. *European Journal of Internal Medicine*

Importantly new examination of the teeth shows that there are no traces of gun powder, indicating that Hitler shot himself through the head -not his mouth. There are, however, blue deposits on the false teeth, which Charlier says demonstrates "a chemical reaction between the cyanide and the metal of the dentures."

"We didn't know if he had used an ampule of cyanide to kill himself or whether it was a bullet in the head," Charlier reported. "It's in all probability both."

CHAPTER NINETEEN

THE NAZIS WHO DID ESCAPE

Historians say that Hitler died in his bunker after shooting himself -but in reality, some Nazis did escape to South America.

Adolph Eichmann

The evil mastermind behind the "final solution" escaped to Argentina in 1950 after hiding out in Austria. He was captured in 1960 by Israeli agents before being hanged as a war criminal - being handed Israel's only ever use of the death sentence.

Josef Mengele

Known as the "Angel of Death", Mengele was an SS officer who experimented on and tortured prisoners at Auschwitz. The vile beast fled to Paraguay, then Brazil, and managed to elude justice before drowning after suffering a stroke while swimming in 1979.

Walter Rauff

The SS colonel behind mobile gas chambers which killed at least 100,000 people during World War II. He managed to escape a prison camp before fleeing to Chile, where he lived out his days until 1984 under the protection of dictator Augusto Pinochet.

Franz Stangl

He was known as "The White Death" for his white uniform and worked to kill thoses with mental and physical disabilities. Escaping to Brazil in 1951, he was eventually captured and taken back to Germany in 1967 - being found guilty of the mass murder of 900,000 people. He died in 1971.

Gerhard Bohne

Headed up a program to help "purify" the Aryan race which oversaw the slaughter of 200,000 people with incurable conditions. He hid out in Argentina after fleeing there in 1949 but was arrested after he returned to Germany in 1963. He fled to Argentina again while on bail, but then became the first Nazi extradited by Buenos Aires -dying in 1981.

CHAPTER TWENTY

America, a Haven for Hitler's Men

In the early '70s, New York Rep. Elizabeth Holtzman received a confidential tip that American immigration authorities knew of dozens of former Nazis -some implicated in serious war crimes -who were living in the U.S.

Holtzman looked into it and discovered that it was true, and that the formerly named Immigration and Naturalization Service wasn't doing much about it. But that was just the tip of the iceberg, according to investigative reporter Eric Lichtblau.

Eric Lichtblau is an investigative reporter for *The New York Times*. In 2006, he won a Pulitzer Prize with James Risen for their stories on the National Security Agency's secret surveillance of American citizens. In his book, in 2014, *The Nazis Next Door*, Eric Lichtblau reports that thousands of Nazis managed to settle in the United States after World War II, often with the direct assistance of American intelligence officials who saw them as potential spies and informants in the Cold War against the Soviet Union.

Lichtblau says there were whole networks of spy groups around the world made up of Nazis -and they entered the U.S., one by one.

"They sort of had put in their service," Lichtblau tells *Fresh Air*'s Dave Davies. "This was their 'reward' ... for their spy service... coming to the United States and being able to live out their lives basically with anonymity and no scrutiny."

Most Americans knew little about the Nazis among them. And then in 1979, media reports and congressional interest finally spurred the creation of a Nazi-hunting unit with the Justice Department. That prompted the first wave of Nazi-hunting, Lichtblau says.

"You had teams of lawyers and investigators and historians at the Justice Department who began... looking at hundreds and hundreds of names of suspected Nazis and Nazi collaborators who were living all around the country, in Queens, in Baltimore, in Florida and Chicago," he says. And, in some cases, the CIA had scrubbed the Nazis' files, Lichtblau says.

"They actively cleansed their records," Lichtblau says. "They realized that guys who had been involved at senior levels of Nazi atrocities would not pass-through immigration at the INS -and they basically removed a lot of the Nazi material from their files."

Highlights of a NPR interview with the author, Eric Lichtblau:

On the treatment of the Jews after liberation:
Even after the liberation of the camps, they were still prisoners. They were kept under armed guard; they were kept behind barbed wire; they were bunked with Nazi POWs. And in some cases, believe it or not, the Nazis still lorded over them while the Allies ruled the camp.

When I started researching the book, this was a book about the Nazis who fled to America. I really had no intention of looking at the survivors -it seemed sort of irrelevant to what I was doing.

And then the more I got into it, and the more horrified I was by the conditions that the survivors lived in -where you had thousands and thousands of people dying even after the liberation, of disease, of malnutrition. I realized it was relevant to the story because as easy as it was for the Nazis to get into America, it was just as horribly difficult for the Jews and the other survivors to get out of the camps.

It took them months, and in some cases a couple of years, to get out of these displaced-person camps. It made me realize that the liberation that I had learned about years ago was in some sense sort of a mockery.

On Nazis running the camps even after the liberation:

[U.S. Army] Gen. [George] Patton believed that the Nazis were best suited to run these camps. In fact, he openly defied orders from then Gen. [Dwight] Eisenhower, who was in charge of the European forces after the war.

Patton was in charge of the displaced persons camps. Patton had sort of an odd fondness almost for the Nazi prisoners, believe it or not. He believed that they [were] the ones in the best position to efficiently run the camps -and he gave them supervisory approval to basically lord over the Jews and the other survivors.

On Nazis and Nazi collaborators getting visas to the United States:

In the early months, and first few years after the war, beginning in mid-1945, [there were] only a very limited number of immigration visas to get into the United States.

There were many, many thousands of Nazi collaborators who got visas to the United States while the survivors did not —even though they had been, for instance, the head of a Nazi concentration camp. Of all the [Holocaust] survivors in the camps, only a few thousand came in in [the] first year or so. To get a visa was a precious commodity, and there were immigration policymakers in Washington who were on record saying that they didn't think the Jews should be let in because they were "lazy people" or "entitled people" and they didn't want them in.

But there were many, many thousands of Nazi collaborators who got visas to the United States while the survivors did not —even though they had been, for instance, the head of a Nazi concentration camp, the warden at a camp, or the secret police chief in Lithuania who signed the death warrants for people. ...

The bulk of the people who got into the United States —some were from Germany itself, some in fact were senior officers in the

Nazi party under Hitler —but more were the Nazi collaborators.

On U.S. intelligence using Nazis as spies:

There were upwards of a thousand Nazis who were used by U.S. intelligence after the war by the CIA, the FBI, the military and other U.S. intelligence agencies —both in Europe as well as inside the United States, in Latin America, in the Middle East, even a few in Australia. And these were seen as basically cold warriors who served as spies, informants and in other intelligence roles.

On whether it was an official policy to bring in Nazis as spies:

I think it was ad hoc. It was not a formal policy approved by the White House or even [Director Allen] Dulles at the CIA to say, "We are going to actively recruit Nazis, their pasts be damned."

There's no document that I found which gives blanket authority for that. But it grew sort of organically because you had whole networks of Nazi spy groups in Europe... as well as the Middle East and Latin America, and often these guys made it into the United States sort of one by one.

There's very little evidence that [the Nazis] had much to do with each other once they got to the United States.

On the remaining classified documents:

There are still documents that remain classified today about the CIA's relationship with Nazi figures in the '40s and '50s and into the '60s. A lot of these documents have become declassified just in the last 10 or 15 years. ... There are documents that may open up whole new chapters that still remain classified that I'd love to see.

CHAPTER TWENTY-ONE

Adolf Hitler's Secret Agent in CIA

According to a report in Express on 18th February 2019, the CIA employed a high-ranking German official after World War II but he was actually secretly protecting a number of Nazi war criminals at the same time, a documentary reveals.

Paul Dickopf served as an active officer in the SS during World War II but, despite his Nazi connections, after the war, he served as the 4th president of the West German Federal Police force and was later elected president of Interpol, the International Criminal Police Organisation. Declassified files from the National Archives in Washington also revealed that Mr. Dickopf received a number of payments from the CIA between 1965 and 1971 to monitor West German officials as Europe was grasped within the clutches of Cold War politics. He was able to successfully move on from his SS past despite his former Nazi connections being known throughout his post-war career.

However, after his death, it was revealed that Mr. Dickopf had been using the Federal Police as a safe haven for former officials and continuing on Adolf Hitler's legacy. Amazon Prime's "Nazis in the CIA" documentary reveals how Mr. Dickopf kept up appearances. The 2017 series detailed: "The [West] German Federal Police was run for six years by Paul Dickopf.

"A top civil servant, with a seemingly clean record, he claimed he opposed the Nazis. "In 1968 he became head of Interpol – it was his job to fight crime on an international level.

Paul Dickopf was working for the CIA (Image: GETTY/ AMAZON)

Paul Dickopf was the 4th president of the Bundeskriminalamt. He was not only a member of the SS and a Nazi spy but shortly before the end of the war, he switched sides to start working as an agent for the CIA.

Nazis in the CIA

"He was held up as an example to all police in Germany." However, the series revealed how declassified CIA files reveal Mr. Dickopf's secrets. It continued: "After Dickopf's death in 1973, staff searching his files to compile his obituary made an astonishing find. "They discovered documents showing Dickopf as a staunch Nazi.

The documents reveal Dickopf was a Nazi (Image: AMAZON PRIME)

Hitler wanted to replace Christianity with Nazi religion says an expert. "His lifelong lie finally comes to light. "Numerous declassified files can now give an insight into Caravel -Dickopf's CIA code name."

One note about Mr. Dickopf by the head of the CIA read: "'Our relationship with Mr. Dickopf is mainly of a secret nature, the official contacts being used as a cover-up for meetings."

Mr. Dickopf passed on to the CIA information on leading officials as well as on internal affairs of the BKA and other authorities.

CHAPTER TWENTY-TWO

MOCKUPS OF HITLER

In November 1944, a Canadian newspaper published some other mock-ups of Hitler designed by a Canadian artist. The header for the page read: *"Would you know Der Fuehrer's face if he settled in Western Canada?"*.

A Canadian newspaper mock-up, 1944

Towards the end of World War II, U.S. intelligence officials were afraid that the German dictator would flee Germany by assuming a disguise. By 1944 the world identified the man largely by his trademark toothbrush mustache and oily side-slicked hair, so they ordered his portrait to be cloned.

The Office of Strategic Services (OSS), an early version of the CIA set up during World War II, asked Eddie Senz, a New York make-up artist, to produce the altered portraits after D-Day on 6 June 1944. Despite fears that Hitler would attempt to flee Germany, the portraits were never needed.

However, photos of Senz's re-imaginings of Hitler were circulated to Allied Commanders during the War but were not seen by the public until the German magazine, Der Spiegel, discovered and published them in the 1990s. Later the U.S. National Archives in Washington DC released the photos with much better resolution. The following pictures show headshots of *Der Führer* in numerous guises.

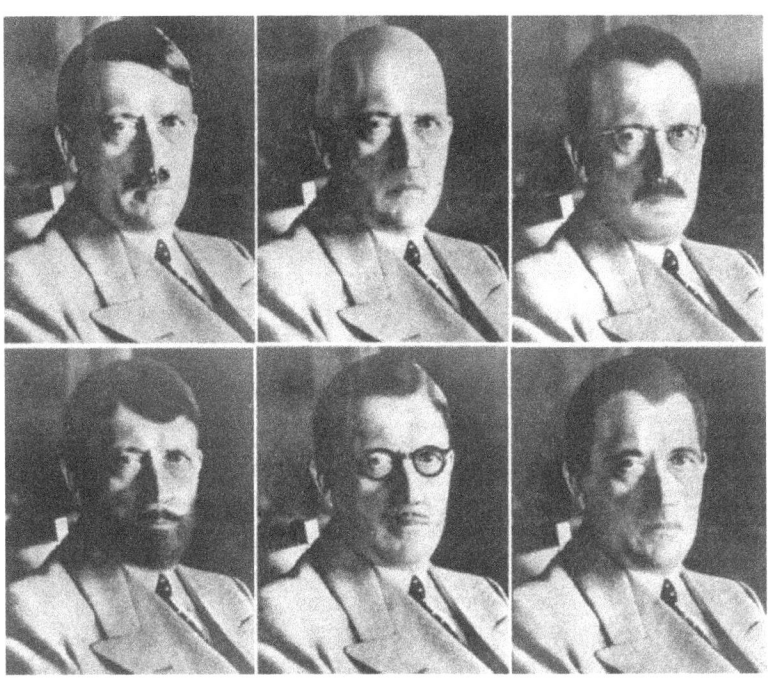

Mockups of Hitler which were produced by wartime intelligence service the OSS (Credit: OSS)

CHAPTER TWENTY-THREE

HITLER FLED WITH US HELP

According to a report in Huffington Post UK, one Abel Basti of the Instituto Florencio Varela in Argentina, claims that the United States helped Hitler escape to South America so that he would not fall into the hands of the Soviet Union.

Basti, who has written extensively on the dictator, told Sputnik News: "There was an agreement with the US that Hitler would run away and that he shouldn't fall into the hands of the Soviet Union. This also applies to many scientists, the military and spies who later took part in the struggle against the Soviet regime."

The historian believes Hitler exited the bunker beneath the Chancellery in Berlin via a tunnel, which took him to Tempelhof Airport, from where a helicopter took him to Spain. From Spain, he traveled to the Canary Islands and then to Argentina in a U-boat.

Hitler spent a decade in Argentina before moving to Paraguay, claims Basti. The former Fuhrer died there on February 3, 1971.

Basti further claims that Hitler was buried in an underground bunker, which is now an elegant hotel in the city of Asuncion. About 40 people attended the burial, and in 1973 the bunker.

Basti's theory of Hitler's escape and route to freedom has been backed by veteran CIA agent Bob Baer.

Baer and his team appeared on History Channel in January, and analysed 700 pages of declassified information, with one stating:

"American Army officials in Germany have not located Hitler's body nor is there any reliable source that Hitler is dead."

In 2009, American researchers claimed that DNA tests on a fragment of Hitler's supposed skull showed that it actually belonged to a woman. The skull with a hole in it was supposedly taken away by the Russians and went on display in Moscow in 2000, where it was considered irrefutable proof of Hitler's suicide. In 2016, archaeologists stumbled upon a 'secret jungle lair' in Argentina, which they believe had been built by Nazis to help their leaders escape Germany if the need arose. But this was unnecessary as then-Argentine president Juan Peron welcomed thousands of Nazis and Italian fascists to the country with open arms.

Joseph Mengele, a doctor who conducted barbaric experiments at the Auschwitz concentration camp and Nazi mastermind Adolf Eichmann lived in Argentina after the Second World War. Eichmann was kidnapped by Israeli agents in 1960, taken to Israel and executed.

In 2000, Argentina issued a formal apology for its history of harbouring Nazi war criminals, but there was no mention of Hitler.

CHAPTER TWENTY-FOUR

THE CIA'S WORST KEPT SECRET?

A report by Martin A. Lee in Foreign Policy in Focus, 1st May, 2001: *"Honest and idealist... enjoys good food and wine... unprejudiced mind..."*

That's how a 1952 Central Intelligence Agency (CIA) assessment described Nazi ideologue Emil Augsburg, an officer at the infamous Wannsee Institute, the SS think tank involved in planning the Final Solution. Augsburg's SS unit performed "special duties," a euphemism for exterminating Jews and other "undesirables" during the Second World War.

Although he was wanted in Poland for war crimes, Augsburg managed to ingratiate himself with the U.S. CIA, which employed him in the late 1940s as an expert on Soviet affairs. Recently released CIA records indicate that Augsburg was among a rogue's gallery of Nazi war criminals recruited by U.S. intelligence agencies shortly after Germany surrendered to the Allies.

Pried loose by Congress, which passed the Nazi War Crimes Disclosure Act three years ago, a long-hidden trove of once-classified CIA documents confirms one of the worst-kept secrets of the cold war–the CIA's use of an extensive Nazi spy network to wage a clandestine campaign against the Soviet Union.

The CIA reports show that U.S. officials knew they were subsidizing numerous Third Reich veterans who had committed horrible crimes against humanity, but these atrocities were overlooked as the anti-Communist crusade acquired its own momentum. For Nazis who would otherwise have been charged with war crimes, signing on with American intelligence enabled them to avoid a prison term.

"The real winners of the cold war were Nazi war criminals, many of whom were able to escape justice because the East and West became so rapidly focused after the war on challenging each other," says Eli Rosenbaum, director of the Justice Department's Office of Special Investigations and America's chief Nazi hunter. Rosenbaum serves on a Clinton-appointed Interagency Working Group (IWG) committee of U.S. scholars, public officials, and former intelligence officers who helped prepare the CIA records for declassification.

Many Nazi criminals "received light punishment, no punishment at all, or received compensation because Western spy agencies considered them useful assets in the cold war," the IWG team stated after releasing 18,000 pages of redacted CIA material. (More installments are pending.)

These are "not just dry historical documents," insists former congresswoman Elizabeth Holtzman, a member of the panel examining the CIA files. As far as Holtzman is concerned, the CIA papers raise critical questions about American foreign policy and the origins of the cold war.

The decision to recruit Nazi operatives had a negative impact on U.S.-Soviet relations and set the stage for Washington's tolerance of human rights abuses and other criminal acts in the name of anti-Communism. With that fateful sub-rosa embrace, the die was cast for a litany of antidemocratic CIA interventions around the world.

The Gehlen Org:

The key figure on the German side of the CIA-Nazi tryst was General Reinhard Gehlen, who had served as Adolf Hitler's top anti-Soviet spy. During World War II, Gehlen oversaw all German military-intelligence operations in Eastern Europe and the USSR.

As the war drew to a close, Gehlen surmised that the U.S.-Soviet alliance would soon break down. Realizing that the United States did not have a viable cloak-and-dagger apparatus in Eastern Europe, Gehlen surrendered to the Americans and pitched himself as someone who could make a vital contribution to the forthcoming struggle against the Communists. In addition to sharing his vast espionage archive on the USSR, Gehlen promised that he could resurrect an underground network of battle-hardened, anti-Communist assets who were well placed to wreak havoc throughout the Soviet Union and Eastern Europe.

Although the Yalta Treaty stipulated that the United States must give the Soviets all captured German officers who had been involved in "eastern area activities," Gehlen was quickly spirited off to Fort Hunt in Virginia. The image he projected during 10 months of negotiations at Fort Hunt was, to use a bit of espionage parlance, a "legend"–one that hinged on Gehlen's false claim that he was never really a Nazi, but was dedicated, above all, to fighting Communism. Those who bit the bait included future CIA director Allen Dulles, who became Gehlen's biggest supporter among American policy wonks.

Gehlen returned to West Germany in the summer of 1946 with a mandate to rebuild his espionage organization and resume spying on the East at the behest of American intelligence. The date is significant as it preceded the onset of the cold war, which, according to standard U.S. historical accounts, did not begin until a year later. The early courtship of Gehlen by American intelligence suggests that Washington was in a cold war mode sooner than most people realize. The Gehlen gambit also belies the prevalent Western notion that aggressive Soviet policies were primarily to blame for triggering the cold war.

Based near Munich, Gehlen proceeded to enlist thousands of Gestapo, Wehrmacht, and SS veterans. Even the vilest of the vile–the senior bureaucrats who ran the central administrative apparatus of the Holocaust–were welcome in the "Gehlen Org," as it was called–including Alois Brunner, Adolf Eichmann's chief deputy. SS major Emil Augsburg and Gestapo captain Klaus Barbie, otherwise known as the "Butcher of Lyon," were among those who did double duty for Gehlen and U.S. intelligence. "It seems that in the Gehlen headquarters, one SS man paved the way for the next, and Himmler's elite were having happy reunion ceremonies," the *Frankfurter Rundschau* reported in the early 1950s.

Bolted lock, stock, and barrel into the CIA, Gehlen's Nazi-infested spy apparatus functioned as America's secret eyes and ears in central Europe. The Org would go on to play a major role within NATO, supplying two-thirds of raw intelligence on the Warsaw Pact countries. Under CIA auspices, and later as head of the West German secret service until he retired in 1968, Gehlen exerted considerable influence on U.S. policy toward the Soviet bloc. When U.S. spy chiefs desired an off-the-shelf style of nation tampering, they turned to the readily available Org, which served as a subcontracting syndicate for a series of ill-fated guerrilla air drops behind the Iron Curtain and other harebrained CIA rollback schemes.

Sitting Ducks for Disinformation:

It's long been known that top German scientists were eagerly scooped up by several countries, including the United States, which rushed to claim these high-profile experts as spoils of World War II. Yet all the while the CIA was mum about recruiting Nazi spies. The U.S. government never officially acknowledged its role in launching the Gehlen organization until more than half a century after the fact.

Handling Nazi spies, however, was not the same as employing rocket technicians. One could always tell whether Werner von Braun and his bunch were accomplishing their assignments for NASA and other U.S. agencies. If the rockets didn't fire properly, then the scientists would be judged accordingly. But how does one determine if a Nazi spy with a dubious past is doing a reliable job?

Third Reich veterans often proved adept at peddling data—much of it false—in return for cash and safety, the IWG panel concluded. Many Nazis played a double game, feeding scuttlebutt to both sides of the East-West conflict and preying upon the mutual suspicions that emerged from the rubble of Hitler's Germany.

General Gehlen frequently exaggerated the Soviet threat in order to exacerbate tensions between the superpowers. At one point he succeeded in convincing General Lucius Clay, military governor of the U.S. zone of occupation in Germany, that a major Soviet war mobilization had begun in Eastern Europe. This prompted Clay to dash off a frantic, top-secret telegram to Washington in March 1948, warning that war "may come with dramatic suddenness."

Gehlen's disinformation strategy was based on a simple premise: the colder the cold war got, the more political space for Hitler's heirs to maneuver. The Org could only flourish under cold war conditions; as an institution, it was therefore committed to perpetuating the Soviet-American conflict.

"The agency loved Gehlen because he fed us what we wanted to hear. We used his stuff constantly, and we fed it to everyone else—the Pentagon, the White House, the newspapers. They loved it, too. But it was hyped-up Russian bogeyman junk, and it did a lot of damage to this country," a retired CIA official told author Christopher Simpson, who also serves on the IGW review panel and was the author of *Blowback: America's Recruitment of Nazis and Its Effects on the Cold War*.

Unexpected Consequences:

Members of the Gehlen Org were instrumental in helping thousands of fascist fugitives escape via "ratlines" to safe havens abroad—often with a wink and a nod from U.S. intelligence officers. Third Reich expatriates and fascist collaborators subsequently emerged as "security advisors" in several Middle Eastern and Latin

American countries, where ultra-right-wing death squads persist as their enduring legacy. Klaus Barbie, for example, assisted a succession of military regimes in Bolivia, where he taught soldiers torture techniques and helped protect the flourishing cocaine trade in the late 1970s and early '80s.

CIA officials eventually learned that the Nazi old boy network nesting inside the Gehlen Org had an unexpected twist to it. By bankrolling Gehlen, the CIA unknowingly laid itself open to manipulation by a foreign intelligence service that was riddled with Soviet spies. Gehlen's habit of employing compromised ex-Nazis–and the CIA's willingness to sanction this practice–enabled the USSR to penetrate West Germany's secret service by blackmailing numerous agents.

Ironically, some of the men employed by Gehlen would go on to play leading roles in European neofascist organizations that despise the United States. One of the consequences of the CIA's ghoulish alliance with the Org is evident today in a resurgent fascist movement in Europe that can trace its ideological lineage back to Hitler's Reich, through Gehlen operatives, who collaborated with U.S. intelligence.

Slow to recognize that their Nazi hired guns would feign an allegiance to the Western alliance as long as they deemed it tactically advantageous, CIA officials invested far too much in Gehlen's spooky Nazi outfit. "It was a horrendous mistake, morally, politically, and also in very pragmatic intelligence terms," says American University professor Richard Breitman, chairman of the IWG review panel.

More than just a bungled spy caper, the Gehlen debacle should serve as a cautionary tale at a time when post-cold war triumphalism and arrogant unilateralism are rampant among U.S. officials. If nothing else, it underscores the need for the United States to confront some of its own demons now that unreconstructed cold warriors are again riding top saddle in Washington.

CHAPTER TWENTY-FIVE

The National Police Gazette: Hitler in Antarctica

On July 13, 2011, Pulp International published an article on Hitler's possible hideout in Antarctica, as claimed by The National Police Gazette, an American magazine founded in 1845 and a forerunner of modern tabloid/sensational journalism. It reads:
THERE GOES THAT MAN AGAIN
Just when you think you've seen the last of this guy, he turns up yet again. Well, here we go again with The National Police Gazette and der Führer. This July 1953 issue brings us to eleven covers we've shared of one of history's biggest monsters. We have seven

more in our archive, and there are certainly others out there in the world to be unearthed. It makes a sort of sense, we suppose that a person who irreparably warped the course of the twentieth century also warped the Gazette's editorial content. In this case, Gazette purports to have located his secret hideout. Where is it? Would you believe Antarctica? No, seriously. They claim that, as of 1953, Hitler was chilling with penguins on an ice shelf. Oooo -march-off! Penguin's win!

Anyway, this is from the Gazette's text: "Hitler is alive! Hitler is plotting to return! These are facts Police Gazette has investigated and fearlessly revealed during recent months. [snip] Why doesn't the United States government take immediate action on our information -track down Hitler, arrest him, and bring him to trial? The answer is this. Our government's hands are tied. We are a democratic nation, and we cannot trespass upon, invade, or interfere with the territorial integrity of another country." Is it not revealing that the Gazette -a rightwing scandal sheet -informs its readers that a murderer of millions must be captured and brought to trial? And that bit about the United States, being a democratic nation that cannot simply invade another country? That's really something, isn't it? Oh, how times change. But we digress. We're wondering if Hitler possibly appeared on more Police Gazette covers than any other person. No way to research that, so we'll just speculate -yes, he did. But in Gazette's defense, it never presented him as anything other than an object of fear or ridicule. At least, not that we've seen. We'll have more Gazette later, and you can get the Antarctic scoop below.

INSIDE HITLER'S SECRET HIDEOUT

Police Gazette reveals inside story of Der Fuehrer's hidden Shangri-La in vast wilderness of the Antarctic.

by George McGrath

This map of the Antarctic Continent shows Queen Maud Land, which the Nazi exploration expedition surveyed and photographed in 1939 as the most likely area in which to build Hitler's new Berchtesgaden. The swastika marks the approximate spot where Hitler's hideout is believed to be.

Antarctica, Police Gazette, Adolf Hitler, Ezzard Charles, Nazis, Tabloid

CHAPTER TWENTY-SIX

The Case of Heinrich Himmler

In 2012, the International Business Times published an interview with Mathias Tietke, a German author, editor, and yoga enthusiast and an expert on German history to explore Himmler and Hinduism.

Among the most interesting and perplexing aspects of the Nazi regime was its connection to India and Hinduism. Indeed, Hitler took the most prominent symbol of ancient India -the swastika as his own.

The link between Nazi Germany and ancient India, however, goes deeper than the swastika symbol. The Nazis venerated the notion of a "pure, noble Aryan race," who are believed to have invaded India thousands of years ago and established a society based on a rigid social structure, or castes.

While scholars in India and Europe have rejected the notion of an "Aryan race, the myths and legends of ancient Vedic-Hindu India have imparted a tremendous influence on Germany.

Perhaps the most fervent Nazi adherent to Indian Hindu traditions was Heinrich Himmler, one of the most brutal members of the senior command.

Himmler, responsible for the deaths of millions of Jews as the architect of the Holocaust, was a highly complex and fascinating man. He was also obsessed with India and Hinduism.

As early as 1925, when Himmler was only 24 years old and had joined the SS, and just two years after Adolf Hitler's beer hall putsch, Himmler wrote: Kshatriyakaste, that is how we need to be. This is salvation. ["Kshatriyakaste" referred to the military and ruling elite of the Vedic-Hindu social system of ancient India.]

Himmler was deeply influenced by the Indologist, yoga scholar, and SS Capt. Jakob Wilhelm Hauer of the University of Tübingen in Germany and the Italian philosopher Baron Julius Evola.

Himmler had a keen interest in the Rigveda and the Bhagavad Gita. According to his personal massage therapist, Felix Kersten, Himmler carried a copy of the Bhagavad Gita in his pocket from 1941 until his death four years later. The book was a translation by the German theosophist, Dr. Franz Hartmann.

The fascination with and admiration of Indian culture can be found as early as the 19th century in the writings of pro-Aryan and anti-Semitic German philosophers and theosophists -always in relation to Indian classical texts.

In 1844, the German philosopher Friedrich Wilhelm Joseph Schelling highlighted in his lectures the same passage from the fourth chapter of the Bhagavad Gita, which 100 years later would fascinate Himmler —so much so that he dictated this passage to his massage therapist. This passage emphasizes that a person's identity does not have to be defined by one's actions -that is, even if they commit evil acts, they can still remain untainted and unaffected by ones' own actions.

Moreover, in 1851, the German philosopher Arthur Schopenhauer raved about the enthusiastic spirit of the Vedas and the Upanishads, citing that his spirit is washed clean of all his early inoculated Jewish superstitions.

Himmler read translations of Indian texts from well-known German and Austrian Indologists. Himmler had clear preferences with some of the scriptures of Hinduism. One was his interest in the Rig Veda, which in some places is imbued with much violence.

The other was the Bhagavad Gita, which he greatly admired and appreciated. Himmler particularly referred to Krishna's instructions on satisfying one's duty on the battlefield and not to identify with such actions.

In a poem written by Himmler, which I discovered in the Federal Archive in Koblenz, he tells stories about the holy life [that] unfolds itself on deadly born.

For the period after the war, the Reichsführer-SS Himmler was already planning a retreat. He recommended that there should be sour milk and brown bread as physical food for his men and the Bhagavad Gita as spiritual nourishment and as the subject for meditation.

Aside from millions of Jews, Himmler was also responsible for the mass murder of up to half-million Roma (Gypsies). Did he not realize that the Roma are of Indian descent themselves?

Himmler even killed his own comrades or SS officers, if, in his view, it served the supposedly higher cause, i.e., the ideology of National Socialism.

Himmler was not really sympathetic so much to the complexities of Indian culture, but rather to the ideal of the Kshatriya [warrior caste of India] and to the ideals of purity.

The Bhagavad Gita is partially about the adventures of Arjuna, the world's greatest warrior.

There are such statements to confirm that Himmler fantasized that he was a 20th-century version of Arjuna "fighting for the glory of the Aryans"

In fact, in an effort to explain his murderous violence, Himmler told his massage therapist Kersten that it would naturally be more pleasant to deal with the flower beds, instead of the sweepings pile and the garbage disposal of the state-- but without that garbage collection, the flower beds would not flourish."

There were statements by Himmler in which he described Hitler as an incarnation of great shining light, as a predestined karma of the Germanic world. Indeed, Himmler equated Hitler with Krishna.

In the Bhagavad Gita, Krishna declared that he will always be reborn when the peoples' sense of right and truth disappeared, and injustice ruled the world. Himmler commented that this verse related directly to Hitler.

"Long Live Germany!" April 1936 [Poster, National Socialist, Nazi]

Himmler conceived of the SS as a kind of "spiritual" order. He demanded loyalty, moral integrity, and also required that his men never acted from base motives.

However, he also required his men to have a pure conscience -inwardly cold, sober, and willing to kill for a higher purpose.

What Himmler had sought and found in yoga was legitimacy, relieving his conscience and overcoming his doubts.

The concept of purity is found both in the writings of yoga as well as in the ideology of National Socialism -that is, the idea that one has to detach oneself from such concepts as "good" and "bad."

The Bhagavad Gita was for Himmler and also for top Nazi ideologue Alfred Rosenberg an important source of inspiration and legitimacy. They could refer to an ancient and sacred text to which British-German philosopher Houston Stewart Chamberlain and German philosopher Friedrich Nietzsche had already referred to. In their comments they wrote of the "Aryan race" and the "Aryan belief" (Chamberlain) and about the superman (Übermensch), the [lower caste] Sudras as the servant race and the degenerates of all caste and about the eject materials in perpetuity (Nietzsche).

During World War II, there was a community of Indian nationalists living in Berlin. The most prominent of these was Subhash Chandra Bose, who met with many top Nazi officials, including Himmler, Joachim von Ribbentrop, Hermann Goering, and Hitler himself. Is it true that Himmler was genuinely interested in helping Bose achieve independence for India (whereas most of the other German leaders only used Bose as a ploy to stoke anti-British sentiments in India)?

Himmler did not have a genuine interest in the independence struggles of India. However, he agreed with Bose's requests to allow for participation in a police training course of selected Indian soldiers in Germany. Since Bose was fascinated by the Nazi police force, including the SS and the Gestapo, whilst in Berlin in July 1942, he asked Himmler personally to train Indians accordingly.

One year earlier, Nazi propaganda minister Josef Goebbels wrote in his diary: Bose is in the Indian question currently, the best horse in our barn.

CHAPTER TWENTY-SEVEN

THE NAZI EXPEDITION TO TIBET

The Germans sent an official expedition to Tibet between 1938 and 1939 at the invitation of the Tibetan Government to attend the Losar (New Year) celebrations.

Tibet had suffered a long history of Chinese attempts to annex it and British failure to prevent the aggression or to protect Tibet. Under Stalin, the Soviet Union was severely persecuting Buddhism, specifically the Tibetan form as practiced among the Mongols within its borders and in its satellite, the People's Republic of Mongolia (Outer Mongolia). In contrast, Japan was upholding Tibetan Buddhism in Inner Mongolia, which it had annexed as part of Manchukuo, its puppet state in Manchuria. Claiming that Japan was Shambhala, the Imperial Government was trying to win the support of the Mongols under its rule for an invasion of Outer Mongolia and Siberia to create a pan-Mongol confederation under Japanese protection.

The Tibetan Government was exploring the possibility of also gaining protection from Japan in the face of the unstable situation. Japan and Germany had signed an Anti-Commintern Pact in 1936, declaring their mutual hostility toward the spread of international Communism. The invitation for the visit of an official delegation from Nazi Germany was extended in this context. In August 1939, shortly after the German expedition to Tibet, Hitler broke his pact with Japan and signed the Nazi-Soviet Pact. In September, the Soviets defeated the Japanese who had invaded Outer Mongolia in May. Subsequently, nothing ever materialized from the Japanese and German contacts with the Tibetan Government.

Ernst Schäfer, a German hunter and biologist, participated in two expeditions to Tibet, in 1931–1932 and 1934–1936, for sport and zoological research. The Ahnenerbe sponsored him to lead a third expedition (1938–1939) at the official invitation of the Tibetan Government. The visit coincided with renewed Tibetan contacts with Japan. A possible explanation for the invitation is that the Tibetan Government wished to maintain cordial relations with the Japanese and their German allies as a balance against the British and Chinese. Thus, the Tibetan Government welcomed the German expedition at the 1939 New Year (Losar) celebration in Lhasa.

In a Research Expedition through Tibet to Lhasa, the Holy City of the God Realm (1950), Ernst Schäfer, described his experiences during the expedition. During the festivities, he reported, the Nechung Oracle warned that although the Germans brought sweet presents and words, Tibet must be careful: Germany's leader is like a dragon. Tsarong, the pro-Japanese former head of the Tibetan military, tried to soften the prediction. He said that the Regent had heard much more from the Oracle, but he himself was unauthorized to divulge the details. The Regent prays daily for no war between the British and the Germans, since this would have terrible consequences for Tibet as well. Both countries must understand that all good people must pray the same. During the rest of his stay in Lhasa, Schäfer met often with the Regent and had a good rapport.

The Germans were highly interested in establishing friendly relations with Tibet. Their agenda, however, was slightly different from that of the Tibetans. One of the members of the Schäfer expedition was the anthropologist Bruno Beger, who was responsible for racial research. Having worked with H. F. K. Günther on Die nordische Rasse bei den Indogermanen Asiens

(The Northern Race among the Indo-Germans of Asia), Beger subscribed to Günther's theory of a "northern race" in Central Asia and Tibet. In 1937, he had proposed a research project for Eastern Tibet and, with the Schäfer expedition, planned to investigate scientifically the racial characteristics of the Tibetan people. While in Tibet and Sikkim on the way, Beger measured the skulls of three hundred Tibetans and Sikkimese and examined some of their other physical features and bodily marks. He concluded that the Tibetans occupied an intermediary position between the Mongol and European races, with the European racial element showing itself most pronouncedly among the aristocracy.

Beger recommended that the Tibetans could play an important role after the final victory of the Third Reich. They could serve as an allied race in a pan-Mongol confederation under the aegis of Germany and Japan. Although Beger also recommended further studies to measure all the Tibetans, no further expeditions to Tibet were undertaken.

Several postwar studies on Nazism and the Occult, such as Trevor Ravenscroft in The Spear of Destiny (1973), have asserted that under the influence of Haushofer and the Thule Society, Germany sent annual expeditions to Tibet from 1926 to 1943. Their mission was first to find and then to maintain contact with the Aryan forefathers in Shambhala and Agharti, hidden subterranean cities beneath the Himalayas. Adepts there were the guardians of secret occult powers, for creating an Aryan master race.

CHAPTER TWENTY-EIGHT

SAVITRI DEVI: THE PRIESTESS OF NAZI

Maximiani Julias Portas was fluent in many languages, English, French, Italian, German, Hindi, Bengal as she taught herself Modern Greek, had knowledge of Ancient Greek, Urdu, and several others. Portas acquired two Master's degrees in philosophy and chemistry then a Ph.D. in philosophy from the University of Lyon, France. She wrote many books in her lifetime praising Nazi ideology and Depicting Hitler as an avatar of Hindu god Vishnu.

From Nazism to Hinduism:

She travelled to Athens, Greece in 1923 at the same time when thousands of refugees were misplaced at the time of Greece's Military Campaign in Asia Minor at the end of World War I. After Greece's humiliation and the Treaty of Versailles. She blamed it all on western allies and in her mind, Greece and Germany were both victims that led her to be a National Socialist. In 1928, Portas renounced her French citizenship, and then she acquired the Greek nationality. Then she embraced national socialism in Palestine after joining a pilgrimage during Lent in the year of 1929 and she was already fascinated by the idea of Aryan purification and eradication of Jews from Europe brought by Hitler's Nazi. Portas blamed Judeo-Christianity for destroying the glory of pure Aryans. She sailed for India in the early 1930s as she believed it is the homeland of pure Aryans and a living version of Europe's pagan past, convinced by the misconceptions of the caste system and forbidden intermarriage. She settled in Calcutta and started working for Hindu Nationalist Movement. While She was studying in Shanti Niketan Ashram she replaced her name with Savitri Devi and then got herself converted into Hinduism. In 1937 she met Shrimat Swami Satyanand, president of the Hindu mission in Calcutta and he offered her service to the mission.

Espionage and Post-War Activities:

In 1939, Savitri Devi met a Bengali brahmin Asit Krishna Mukherjee, the editor of New Mercury a Nazi mouthpiece funded by the German consulate living in Calcutta. Savitri Devi claimed that Mukherjee knew Subhas Chandra Bose well and it was their contacts in the Japanese legation that Bose got touch with and with whom he collaborated between 1943 to 1945. She also distributed pro-axis propaganda and she got engaged in intelligence gathering on the British in India. After her marriage, she and her husband continued spying and gathering intelligence for the axis cause. The info was then passed on to the Japanese which was useful and resulted in successful launched military attacks against allied airbases and military units. After the defeat of Axis powers, she was devastated, and she travelled to Europe again and vowed that she would do what she could to uphold the Nazi ideology. In 1945 She left India and went to Germany where she distributed thousands of copies of handwritten leaflets encouraging men and women to have faith in national socialism and resist, but she got arrested for posting bills and got tried in 1949 for the promotion of Nazi ideas on German territory. There she was sentenced to two years and after eight months imprisonment, she was released and expelled from Germany. After returning and visiting Germany she acquainted with neo-Nazi fascists from all over Europe and started participating in various conferences and activities.

CHAPTER TWENTY-NINE

LIFE AFTER DEATH?

One of the persons who responded to the Notification issued by the Justice Mukherjee Commission of Inquiry (1999-2005), the third of its kind, on Netaji's death and disappearance, in accordance with Rule 5(2)(b) of the Commissions of Inquiry (Central) Rules 1972 by filing a statement (supported by an affidavit) was Shri Jagannath Prosad Gupta, a resident of village Nagda In the district of Sheopurkalan (Madhya Pradesh). He asserted that during the days of struggle for freedom of India a plane crash-landed in the neighbouring village of Pandola and the three persons who survived the crash were a 'Sadhu', Col Habibur Rahman, and Hitler. Later on, the 'Sadhu came to their village and started living on the bank of the river nearby. The 'Sadhu' who carried the name of Jyotirdev used to correspond regularly with the senior officers and used to go out of the village frequently. According to Shri Gupta, he was none other than Netaji and he died on May 21, 1977, in Sheopurkalan. He stated that after his death the Government of Madhya Pradesh had seized all records pertaining to the 'Sadhu' and, according to him, those documents contained proof of his identity as Netaji. Three affidavits sworn by Ram Bharosi Sharma of village Nagda, Karlar Singh of village Raipura, and Gurdayal Singh of village Mohana were filed in support of Shri Gupta's statement.

A Japanese newspaper, published on 23 August 1945 reported the death of Netaji Subhas Chandra Bose

In course of the inquiry, the Commission examined all the above four persons at Sheopurkalan (CWs 26, 27, 29, and 30). Besides, Mrs. Dulari Bai of village Nagda, whose association with the "Sadhu' transpired during the examination of the above witnesses, was also examined (CW 28). The statements of these five witnesses undoubtedly prove that a 'Sadhu' by the name Jyotirdev.

lived in the district of Sheopurkalan for quite a number of years and that he died there on May 21, 1977, but their claim that the 'Sadhu' was Netaji is wholly unfounded. Admittedly, none of them saw Netaji earlier nor are the documents filed by them have any relevance to the issue. Besides, the documents seized by the police from the residence of the 'Sadhu' after his death at the instance of Shri Gupta did not at all support his contention that those documents would unmistakably prove that the 'Sadhu' was Netaji, so far as the story of a plane crash in 1946 is concerned, it is patently absurd. For the foregoing reasons the claim of the above five witnesses that Netaji died at Sheopurkaian on May 21, 1977, has got to be rejected outright.

The JMCI during its course of the inquiry, among other possibilities, considered the Gumnami-Baba alias Bhagwanji angle. Though Justice Mukherjee, in the report, nixed the air crash theory, he did not conclude that the `Sanyasi` was Bose due to the "Absence" of any clinching evidence.Incidentally, a documentary "Black Box of History" made by Mr. Amlan Kusum Ghosh on the Netaji mystery, has footage (accidentally taken without Justice Mukherjee`s knowledge) in which the retired judge is heard saying: "I am 100 percent sure that he (the monk) is Netaji."

Speculations linking Gumnami Baba alias Bhagwanji -Netaji Subhas Chandra Bose got a boost at the Faizabad district treasury in 2016, when inland letters and telegrams written by and received from Dr. Pabitra Mohan Roy (senior official of Bose's Indian National Army's intelligence wing) surfaced among the belongings of Bhagwanji at Ram Bhawan, Faizabad where he lived the final years.

> **WAR DEPARTMENT**
> MILITARY INTELLIGENCE SERVICE
> WASHINGTON
>
> MID 915
>
> ID/CG/WLB
> WFZ/mcs
>
> 20 June 1946
>
> MEMORANDUM FOR: Mr. Jack D. Neal, Chief
> Division of Foreign Activity Correlation
> Department of State
> Washington 25, D. C.
>
> SUBJECT: Subhas Chandra Bose, Request for Information regarding
>
> 1. A search of the files in the Intelligence Division reveals that there is no direct evidence that SUBHAS CHANDRA BOSE was killed in an airplane crash at Taihoko, Formosa, despite the public statement of the Japanese to that effect. Nor is there any evidence available to Intelligence Division which would indicate that the subject is still alive.
>
> 2. Possibly a determination of the facts in this matter could be made by G-2 of the Supreme Commander for the Allied Powers, in Tokyo. It is believed that a request for such information could properly be made through the British representative to the Allied Control Council-Japan.
>
> FOR THE CHIEF, COLLECTION GROUP:
>
> Ralph E. Curtiss
> RALPH E. CURTISS
> Lieut. Colonel, Inf.
> Chief, Washington Liaison Branch

Inquiry Report of the War Department (PC: Anuj Dhar)

In all, 197 items probed by Justice Mukherjee Commission were viewed. A letter dated September 16, 1972, written by former Rashtriya Swayamsevak Sangh (RSS) second chief (Sarsanghchalak) M.S. Golwalkar was also retrieved. Golwalkar, in his letter addressed Bhagwanji as 'Pujyapad Shrimaan Swami

Vijayanandji Maharaj'. The letter written by Golwalkar read, "I received your letter written from August 25 to September 2 on September 6, 1972. If you pin-point one particular location out of the three places mentioned in the letter, then my job will certainly become easier."

BBC Report on the Taiwanese reply to Justice Mukherjee

Guru Golwalkar's letter to Bhagwanji (PC: Times of India)

Paying his respect to Baba, Golwalkar also says, "I derive strength from the concerns and thoughts, which are crisscrossing your mind. And I am confident that this will eventually help to resolve all the problems."

Did second Sarsanghchalak of RSS, M.S. Golwalkar know who Gumnami Baba alias Bhagwanji really was?

RSS' fifth chief K.S. Sudarshan in his speech in Kolkata, on April 23, 2005, claimed that Netaji did not die in the Taihuku plane crash, was alive till 1985. The Sangh chief also demanded that the Justice Mukherjee Commission be sent to Russia by the then UPA government to examine the documents associated with him.

A letter written by him on June 7, 2007, addressed to Shakti Singh, the owner of Ram Bhawan categorically states that the news of Netaji's death in the Taihuku plane crash was "presumed" to be true.

"Netaji Subhas Chandra Bose returned from Russia in or around 1953 and lived as Gumnami Baba in different parts of the nation."

"But the truth is that two of India's ambassadors to Russia, Vijaya Lakshmi Pandit, and S. Radhakrishnan, had met Netaji in person inside the jail in Russia. Both of them were instructed not to spread the news about Bose's survival."

He added that it is because of this neglect that he was forced to lead his life as Gumnami Baba, either in the Himalayas or in and around Ayodhya. Singh said that Sudarshan at times regretted that RSS did not have that strength and could not act in time to help Bose.

It is reported that Bose had the first-hand experience of the RSS, through the window of a train, in which he was traveling. While passing through Maharashtra, he saw the swayamsevaks in uniform parading in the route march. On enquiring about the organisation from which the swayamsevaks belonged, he discovered that the organisation was RSS, and its founder it was none other than his colleague from the Congress party, Dr. Keshav Baliram Hedgewar.

He was curious to observe the discipline and the communion with which the swayamsevaks were marching. He met Dr. Hedgewar in June of 1940 in Nagpur. Scholars argue that Netaji wanted to meet him regarding "an issue of national importance". Another group of scholars argue that Netaji was planning to forge an alliance of the INA and the RSS for joint efforts in the freedom struggle. However, Dr. Hedgewar was seriously ill and was unable to speak. Unfortunately, he passed away on June 21, in the same week in which the two great leaders could meet to talk about the "issue of national importance".

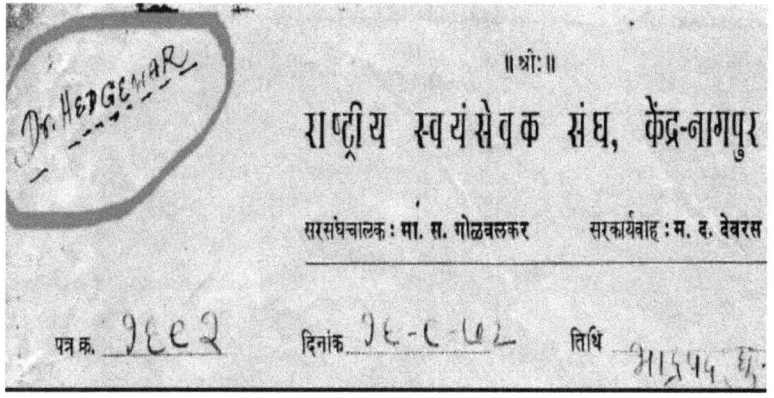

Bhagwanji writes "Dr. HEDGEWAR" on top of the Guru Golwalkar's letter (PC: Anuj Dhar)

Dr. Hedgewar was well connected with the Bengal revolutionaries. He took Doctor's degree from the National Medical College, Calcutta, and passed out in June 1914. He chose Calcutta to carry out his studies because the city was the hub of nationalist revolutionaries. He soon got associated with the freedom movement. The renowned revolutionary, Nalini Kishore Guha, introduced Keshav and Narayanrao Savarkar, younger brother of Veer Savarkar, into the Anusheelan Samity, a secret revolutionary organization, He was given the secret name 'Cocaine' and soon became a prominent revolutionary.

Under the leadership of Bose, the Congress youth group in Bengal was organised into a quasi-military organisation called the Bengal Volunteers. Bose deplored Gandhi's pacifism. Both Bose and Dr. Hedgewar began their public lives as activists of the Indian National Congress. Netaji emerged as the most popular leader of the Congress and Dr. Hedgewar became the Secretary of Vidarbha Congress Committee. Congress heading towards appeasement politics compelled both to leave Congress. Dr. Hedgewar founded the Rashtriya Swayamsevak Sangh (RSS) in Nagpur in 1925 and kept close links with the revolutionary organizations in Punjab and Calcutta. Bose assumed the leadership of the Indian Independence League (IIL) and the Indian National Army (INA) in Singapore in 1943.

After the defeat of Italy and Germany in World War II, Hindu nationalists distanced themselves from the totalitarian regimes of Europe. However, their calls for a Hindu India have only strengthened over the years.

Two years back, the RSS's sixth chief Mohan Bhagwat made a statement at a programme held at Mukherjee University Morabadi, said: "...people should avoid using the word "Nationalism" as its meaning could be seen to be derived from Hitler's Nazism. There is unrest across the country due to fundamentalism, however, every citizen of India is connected to each other despite the diversity in the country because "we are connected with the word Hindu".

However, Nazism, and the mysticism of Adolf Hitler's warped philosophies, remain an obsession with many Indians, after so many years of the Der Führer came to power in Germany.

CHAPTER THIRTY

Nanga Parvata: German Mountain of Destiny in Kashmir region

Nanga Parbat, also called **Diamir**, is one of the world's tallest mountains, 26,660 feet (8,126 meters) high, situated in the western Himalayas 27 km west-southwest of Astor, in the Pakistani-administered sector of the Kashmir region.

The mountain's steep south wall rises nearly 15,000 feet above the valley immediately below, and the north side drops about 23,000 feet to the Indus River.

The British Alpine climber Albert F. Mummery led the first attempt to ascend the glacier- and snow-covered mountain in 1895, but he died in the attempt. At least 30 more climbers (mostly German-led) also perished on Nanga Parbat because of the severe weather conditions and frequent avalanches before the Austrian climber Hermann Buhl reached the top in 1953. The Kashmiri name Nanga Parbat is derived from the Sanskrit words *nagna parvata*, meaning "naked mountain." Diamir is a local name for the peak and means "king of the mountains."

In 1924, in his first "TRUE" BERGFILM (mountain film), German director Dr. Arnold Fanck told the story of a fictional local climber ("The Mountaineer") whose imagination was seized by the idea of scaling the Guglia del Diavolo, supposedly a forbidding rock tower in the Italian Dolomites. Again and again, he attempts the perilous ascent, only to eventually fall to his death. His unfulfilled dream is finally realized by "His Son," who, in the effort of saving his friend Hella during her own illfated attempt on the Guglia, reaches the summit. The title of Fanck's immensely popular mountain drama -a film that for seventy-two days in a row played to sold-out audiences in Berlin -was "Mountain of Destiny" (*Der Berg des Schicksals*).

1953 German-Austrian Nanga Parbat expedition

Less than ten years later, as if following an unintended script, the fictional drama of Fanck's film -with its themes of mountaineering obsession, generational legacy, and ultimate triumph -would begin to play itself out for real, the fictional Guglia del Diavolo replaced by an actual, even more forbidding mountain, and the audiences' fascination with the struggle of man against mountain rising to yet unseen heights. Never before or after, in fact, would a mountain capture the German imagination longer and more thoroughly than Nanga Parbat (from Sanskrit: Nanga Parvata, the "Naked Mountain"), located in the extreme western part of the Himalaya chain located in the Kashmir area at 8,125 meters the world's ninth-highest peak and more than 5,000 kilometres away from Berlin presented no bar to the prominent place it once occupied in the minds of the Germans.

Repeatedly referred to by 1930s mountaineers as the German "mountain of destiny," Nanga Parbat -over a period of roughly two decades between 1932 and 1953 -became not only the destination of six German mountaineering expeditions but also the quintessential German "mountain of the mind" onto whose slopes, German mountaineers, mountaineering officials, politicians, writers, and filmmakers would project some of the most pressing social, political, and cultural concerns of their time.

As Harald Hobusch relates in Mountain of Destiny: Nanga Parbat and its path into the German imagination, it all began when the Schlagintweit brothers, Hermann, Adolph and Robert, explorers and scientists from Munich, embarked on their expedition to India and the Himalayas to conduct a Magnetic Survey of India -a project originally conceived by Alexander von Humboldt. It was Adolph who first drew a panorama of Nanga Parbat in great detail.

CHAPTER THIRTY-ONE

KASHMIR: THE ARYAN VALLEY

The first chapter of *Wars and No Peace Over Kashmir* by M. Maroof Raza reads: The Kashmir Valley is believed to have been a prehistoric lake. Indian mythology maintains that Lord Shiva and his wife Parvati helped in the creation of a dried-up lake and a basin-shaped Valley some 84 miles long and about 25 miles wide. In honour of the great sage Kashyap Muni, who had asked for Shiva's assistance, the Valley was called, Kashyapamar or Kashyapbhumi –and in due course came to be known by the name of Kashmir. Geologists have confirmed that indeed a great lake once existed, and a post-Ice age earthquake shattered the mountains and dried the lake. There is also proof of Kasmir's ancient past in a Sanksrit document of AD 1148 by the poet historian Kalhana, titled *Rajtarangini.* It also tells that the victorious Pandavas of *Mahabharata* took to the Valley, and apparently so did Emperor Ashoka the Great (274 to 237 BC).

Some historians are of opinion that India is the original homeland of the Aryans. They point out that in the subsequent period the Aryans migrated from India to other countries. The river hymns of the Rig Veda mention Ganga, the Yamuna at first and then mention the rivers of Punjab, the Indus, and the rivers of Afghanistan. The geographical order of the names of the rivers indicates their location from the East to the West. It has been pointed out that the river hymn signifies the migration of the Aryans from the Brahmarshi Desha or the Ganga-Yamuna Doab towards the North-West. In course of such migration, they invoked the names of their gods, Indra, Mitra, and Varuna in the Boghaz-koi inscription.

Some 130 km north-east of Kargil, on the Line of Control, there are villages of Dah, Hano (Hano Goma and Hano Yogma), Darchik, and Garkon. These villages are situated on the northern bank of Indus on the road to Baltistan. Here is found a community that for thousands of years have lived in isolation in their inaccessible villages. They have distinct features -tall and statuesque, with green eyes, high cheekbone, fair with flawless skin, and some with blonde hair. They consider themselves to be the pure bloodline of the Aryans. The community also claims to be the direct descendants from the Alexander's Army, some of whom reportedly stayed back after Alexander abandoned his campaign at the banks of river Indus in 326 BC. They are the 1800 strong Brokpa tribe. The community calls itself Minaro (meaning Aryan) but is popularly known as Brokpa. They are part of the Dards some of whom are found in isolated pockets in India and Pakistan Occupied Kashmir (POK) in the Baltistan region. Brokpas have maintained their purity of race and culture without being hostile to the influence of the outside world. Strong social rules and pride in their ancestry have helped preserve their way of life and genetic uniqueness. According to Dr. Veena Bhasin, Professor of Anthropology, the University of Delhi, who has done seminal work on this ethnic group, the tribe has been present in this region of Ladakh for 5000 years. They claim to be the first settlers and trace their migration from Europe to Gilgit and then eventually to their present location. While this is preserved in the folklore, there is no other scientific proof to this claim, and no credible history of the Brokpas has been written.

In his 2006 documentary titled *The Aryan Saga*, Sanjeev Siwan tells the story of German women coming to Brokpa villages to have babies with Brokpa men. These women subscribe to the belief that the Brokpa is the only remaining pure Aryans. In the documentary a German lady is interviewed, who is in Darchik and has a tryst with Tsewang Lhundup, a Brokpa man, with the intent to have his baby. She is candid in admitting that there have been other German women before her and definitely she is not the last one. Tsewang Lhundup is also shown in the film and is quite open about his liaison. Such pregnancy tourism is paid for and is organised. Major HPS Ahluwalia, the first Indian to climb Mt Everest, in his book *Hermit Kingdom Ladakh* (1980) mentions of meeting 'three sophisticated German ladies at a Brokpa festival. They had heard the Aryan stories and were, he says, 'in search of seed'. Kai Fraise in the book *Written for Ever* (edited by Rukun Advani) writes about his search of evidence regarding the phenomenon between the German women and Brokpa men but finds no credible evidence.

The villages are located near the line of control, the fierce 1999 Kargil war disturbed their habitat forever. Because of their inborn capacity for high altitude conditions, they were very useful to the Indian Army. They fought alongside the Army during the war without fearing for their lives. For six months no man in the tribe returned home during the 1999 Kargil War. They helped the Army in locating places, help them know this terrain, help them carry goods, they did all they could to save this country.

It is reported that since the Kargil war, the Rashtra Swayamsevak Sangh (RSS) has become politically active in the Himalayan region to protect what they perceive to be India's natural frontier lines, a task for which Brogpa Aryanism plays an indispensable role. The RSS treats Aryanism and associated Vedic cultures as fundamentally Indian, an ideology that validates India's Hindu origins. In order to disprove theories of Aryan invasions into India, the RSS promotes Brogpas as "pure Aryans," and India's *mul nivasis* or indigenous.

CHAPTER THIRTY-TWO

KASHMIR'S FORGOTTEN CHAPTER

It is not true that Pakistan lent support to the tribal infiltration because it had been precipitated by an internal revolt of the Muslim population of the region. The argument that peasant unrest in Poonch (June to October 1947) triggered a large-scale revolt of the Muslims against the Hindu ruler is untenable -an argument made by Prof. Nandalal Chakrabarti, former Head of the Department of Political Science, Presidency College, Kolkata was published in the 'The Statesman, January 14, 2019.

It reads: On the evening of 24 October 1947, at a dinner party in Delhi, Nehru informed Mountbatten that an invasion of Kashmir by tribesmen from the North West Frontier had taken place. Apprehending imminent danger, the Viceroy called a meeting of the Defence Committee the next morning. General Lockhart, Commander-in-Chief of the Indian Army, reported on the basis of a communication from the Pakistan Army Headquarters in Rawalpindi, that 5000 tribesmen from the North West had entered Kashmir and burnt down the town of Muzaffarabad on their way towards Srinagar. Maharaja Hari Singh, the ruler of Kashmir, made a desperate appeal for help to India. He wrote to Mountbatten on 26 October that tribesmen could not have come in motor trucks using the Mansehra-Muzaffarabad Road fully armed with up-to-date weapons without the knowledge of the Provisional Government of the North West Frontier Province and the Government of Pakistan. Retired officers of the Pakistan Army confirmed that Pakistan had provided logistic support to the tribesmen.

Following the division of the British Indian Army, the bulk of the military assets remained within the Dominion of India in 1947. Those within the Dominion of Pakistan were largely obsolete. How did Pakistan supply modern arms and ammunition to the tribesmen? It is not true that Pakistan lent support to the tribal infiltration because it had been precipitated by an internal revolt of the Muslim population of the region. The argument that peasant unrest in Poonch (June to October 1947) triggered a large-scale revolt of the Muslims against the Hindu ruler is untenable. General Victor Scott, the British Commander-in-Chief of the Kashmir state forces, informed that "in September 1947, the State troops had escorted one lakh Muslims through Jammu territory on their way to Pakistan and an equal number of Sikhs and Hindus going the other way" (General Victor Scott's Report; British Library). Thus, the raiders' objective had hardly anything to do with the bogey of Muslims in danger in Kashmir, a convenient ruse that is proffered by Pakistan to cover up its own agenda of territorial expansion.

What happened in Kashmir in 1947? In the wake of Partition, when communal tension flared up around the state, Hindu-Muslim relations became strained in certain areas. There was unease in Jammu and the frontier adjoining the Pathan tribal areas. And yet, "Kashmir", as stated by the British Resident WP Webb, "remained free from communal disturbances". The region had never allowed the rot to set in despite the instigation of communal outfits from within and outside. As early as 1943, the Muslim League envoy to Kashmir informed Jinnah, "No important religious leader has ever made Kashmir his home or even an ordinary center of Islamic activities. It will require considerable effort, spread over a long period of time, to reform them and convert them into true

Muslims".

Three years later, Agha Shaukat Ali, a Muslim Conference leader in Kashmir, threatened "direct action" to enforce the two-nation agenda but, failed to unite the warring factions of the Muslim Conference. This proves that there was no communal sentiment. Pakistan and its cohorts propagated the view that the tribesmen, driven by their primordial greed and cruel instinct for destruction, looted the state. Sharbaz Khan Mazari, a tribal leader from Baluchistan, in his book A journey to disillusionment, says that he was stopped by Pakistani officials while trying to persuade some men to join the fighting in Kashmir.

As Mazari points out, they thought that "he and his men were intent on partaking in the plunder that was taking place". The reference to the people unleashing the plunder has been made vague and if we go by his own statement, the intention of Mazari and his people was different. Did the Pakistani officials want to hide from the Baluch tribal leader what the military contingent of Pakistan was doing inside Kashmir, to capture the entire region? If it is taken for granted that the tribesman was the saviour of the distressed Muslim brethren, the question remains unresolved as to how the saviour became the looter. Attempts to explain it by citing the greedy and cruel nature of the tribes of the North West have never been convincing. Obviously, they were driven by a motive unrelated to Pakistan's plan of action.

Satya Bakshi, a renowned journalist, and a freedom-fighter wrote in an editorial in "*Socialist Republican*" on 8 November 1947 that INA men like Major General MZ Kiani and Col Habibur Rehman had led the tribesmen into the State of Jammu and Kashmir. Pakistani sources also recorded ex-INA officers' involvement in the raid. V P Menon, the constitutional advisor to Mountbatten, in the magnum opus, Integration of the Indian States", referred to the presence of INA veterans like Md Zaman Kiani and Burhanuddin in the tribal raid. The presence of Burhanuddin makes the entire episode more intriguing. Burhanuddin was the Prince of Chitral who became a Commander of INA in Burma. Chitral, the largest district in the Khyber Pakhtunkhwa previously known as North West Frontier Province, is separated from Tajikistan by a narrow strip of the Wakhan Corridor, which extends from north-eastern Afghanistan to China. According to a British intelligence report of 1946, Nehru received a letter from Bose stating he was in Russia and that he wanted to come to India via Chitral (File No. 223 INA). Did Burhanuddin have any inkling of the plan? It has often been pointed out that Burhanuddin joined the raid because he endorsed Kashmir's accession to Pakistan and supported a Muslim uprising against the ruler of Kashmir, Maharaja Hari Singh, who was inclined towards accession to India. There was speculation too that since he had a strong Islamic orientation, he must have organised the raid with Kiani to free his Muslim brethren from Hindu rule. Nothing can be farther from the truth. On the other hand, if it is argued that Kiani organised the raid because after migrating to Pakistan he was put in charge of the southern wing to overthrow the Government of Jammu and Kashmir, it would only be a half-truth. Kiani did not willingly leave India. He left India because he felt the worst possible disgrace. This will be evident from the Congress leaders' attitude towards the INA.

In an interview with a returned POW, Captain Hari Badhwar on 18 October 1945, Asaf Ali, a member of the Congress Working Committee, said that if the Congress was in power "it would have no hesitation in removing all INA from services" and "if Government now postponed trials, the Congress would put INA leaders on trial when in power". Everybody knows who came to power in India in 1947 and how INA soldiers/ officers were prevented from joining the Indian Army despite cosmetic changes of policy from time to time. They were welcomed by Pakistan and offered opportunities to join the forces. But it would be a gross over-simplification to infer that they opted for the other Dominion. One should not ignore their constraints in India. They would not have been allowed to organise forces to move towards Kashmir for receiving their leader. Neither the British nor the Indian authorities accorded them any locus standi. So, it could have been very much on the cards that these people had an underlying motive different from the occupation of Kashmir by Pakistan.

It is preposterous to assume that Major General Kiani, who was instructed by Subhas Chandra Bose himself to represent the Provisional Government of Azad Hind in his absence, would organise the raid to assist Pakistan's annexation of Kashmir. Whatever have been the front, in all likelihood these men masterminded the raid, receiving the information of Bose's possible return to India through that region. An intelligence report of the Home Department reveals that in 1946 meetings were held in the Northwest Frontier Province demanding the release of all INA men from custody.

INA's connection with the Northwest Frontier is not, therefore, a figment of imagination. Bose himself planned attacks on British forces from the tribal areas of the Northwest. He stated in his memorandum of 9 April 1941 presented in Germany, that "our agents are already working in the independent Tribal territory lying between Afghanistan and India. Their efforts will have to be coordinated and an attack on British military centers will have to be planned on a large scale". (File No L/P and J/12/217: Public Record Office, London). Bhagatram Talwar, one of Bose's aides, brought Sodhi Harminder Singh and Santimoy Ganguly from India in the same year for training in underground combat in Afghanistan. Such circumstantial evidence suggests that the ex-INA men tried to facilitate their leader's safe passage to Kashmir by leading the tribesmen to the Valley to establish a completely free zone there.

Then again, there comes another story of a mysterious Sanyasi behind Kashmir's accession to India. Ramchandra Kak was the Prime Minister from June 30, 1945, to August 11, 1947, when he was sacked, arrested, and tried on false charges. Initially, Maharaja Hari Singh was liberal and free from religious prejudices, but he came under the sway of Swami Sant Dev. When Nehru came to Kashmir for the second time in 1946, he visited him, an old friend (*Selected Works of Jawaharlal Nehru*, First Series, Volume 15; page

418).

Kak writes: The Maharaja believed that after the departure of the British from India, he would through the potency of the Swami's supernatural powers, be able to extend his territory and rule over a much larger dominion than that already comprised in the Jammu and Kashmir State. A good deal of propaganda was being carried on in the State and in Punjab, about the formation of what some people then called Dogristan, in which it was hoped to include, besides the Jammu and Kashmir State, the districts of Kangra and the States and areas now mostly included in Himachal Pradesh. Kak was not forgiven for administering a cold douche to the idea. The Swami was pro-Congress and launched a parallel diplomatic channel. Kak recorded these developments in detail in a note he submitted to Hari Singh on July 30, 1947, which he has reproduced in full in his Note of 1956. The Swami parted company with Hari Singh when they left Srinagar for Jammu.

Kak's version on this episode also is supported, this time, by Dr. Karan Singh (Son of Maharaja Hari Singh) in his autobiography, *Heir Apparent* (Oxford University Press; 37): A strange development took place in our household. A certain Swami Sant Dev, who had lived in the State decades earlier in the time of the late ruler, Maharaja Pratap Singh, and was reported to have been banished by my father when he ascended the throne, staged a mysterious comeback. My father was far from being a religious man, but to everyone's amazement, he suddenly became a devout disciple of Swamiji, sitting for long periods on the ground before him and never smoking in his presence.

Swamiji was presented by him with lovely silk robes, a silver hookah, and many other amenities, including a car. He was a remarkable man in many ways, erudite in several fields of knowledge and pink-complexioned even in his advanced age. He would never actually reveal how old he was, but it was rumoured that he was well over eighty (some claimed a hundred).

It was in the political sphere that Swamiji's influence proved to be disastrous. As with many of the larger Indian States, the prospect of becoming an independent ruler after the British withdrawal was an alluring one for my father. It was on this feudal ambition that Swamiji astutely played, planting in my father's mind visions of an extended kingdom sweeping down to Lahore itself, where our ancestor Maharaja Gulab Singh and his brothers Raja Dhian Singh and Raja Suchet Singh had played such a crucial role a century earlier. There is also some reason to believe that Swamiji was in touch with some of the Congress leaders and that Acharya Kriplani's visit to the State early in 1947 was a direct result of his intervention. Another visitor to Srinagar was A.S.B. Shah, Pakistan's States Minister, who warned the Frontier's Chief Minister, Abdul Qayum, on October 18 that aggression on Kashmir would provoke Hari Singh's accession to India, which it did (R.J. Noore; *Making the New Commonwealth*; Oxford University Press; page 50). Jinnah was fully aware of it. He had heard of it 15 days earlier but preferred not to be told much. Don't tell me anything about it (ibid. page 51). Tacit consent was not concealed.

CHAPTER THIRTY-THREE

Escape Submarine

Then what happened to Bose? Iqbal Chand Malhotra, a documentary filmmaker, and researcher from Delhi are of the firm belief that with World War II ending in favour of the Allied Forces, Netaji made his escape. He did not escape from Saigon on board a Japanese bomber that is supposed to have crashed in Taipei (which is the general belief among those who believe that Netaji survived) but on a German submarine from Singapore that carried him to Vladivostok. From here, Bose made his way to the inland USSR. The submarine, which contained gold and precious stones, then sailed to Tokyo. According to Malhotra, the submarine was part of the 'Monsun group that was deployed in south-east Asia courtesy, the Germans.

The 33rd flotilla was based in Penang and had 34 German U boats and 7 Italian transport submarines. But it continued operations even after the Germans surrendered in May 1945. What happened to Bose after he disembarked at Vladivostok? Purabi Roy, an Indian researcher who spent long years in Russia, came to know about a document in the archives of GRU (an intelligence agency) in Podolsk near Moscow that refers to a meeting between Joseph Stalin and his three aides (Vyacheslav Molotov, Andrey Vyshinsky, and Yakov Malik) in October 1946 where they were discussing 'where to keep Chandra Bose.'

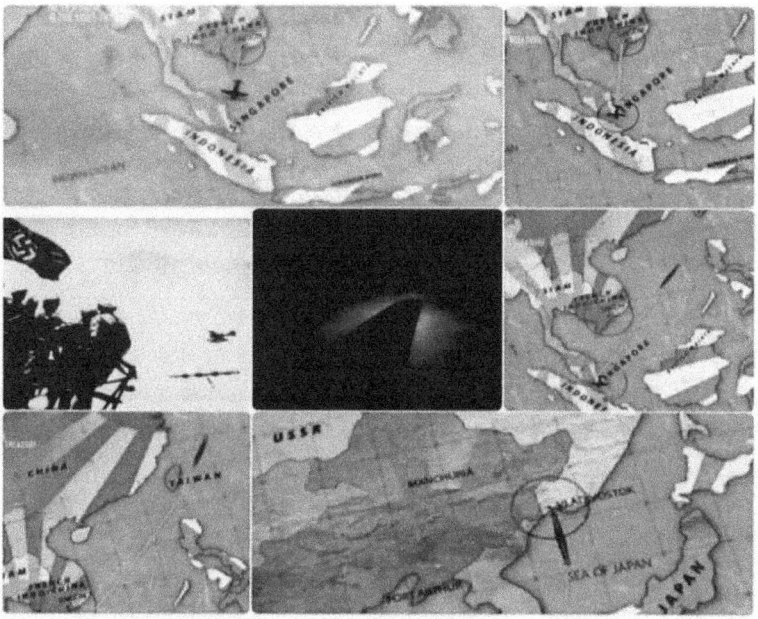

Bose's possible escape route (Courtesy: History TV18)

Towards the end of World War II, many people believe a similar theory that Hitler and other high-ranking Nazi officials escaped Germany via a submarine to flee to South America.

According to Daily Mail, the submarine, specifically called the U-3523, was a high-tech German submarine that had the ability to cruise for extremely long periods of time. The submarine has now been found increasing speculation that Hitler did indeed, escape the furious end to World War II. Jim Saltney reports in PrepForThat: There is n't much debate that the submarine had the ability to make the route from Germany to South America, but what remains in question, and unlikely, according to most historians, is Hitler's place on the submarine. The submarine was designed strategically to traverse the open seas for extended periods of time.

In 1945, the British claimed they shot the U-3523 submarine down. The only issue with this claim is that the wreckage was never discovered. This led many to believe that the submarine stealthy escaped harboring high-ranking Nazis, Hitler included.

But now the theory has been shot down (pun intended) by Denmark's Sea War Museum, the locators of the submarine treasure. The wreckage was located in Northern Denmark, near Skagen. That ends up being nine miles just west of the original attack on it.

The Sea War Museum's director, Gert Normann Andersen, had this to say regarding the find, as well as past conspiracy theories.

Rumour has it that the submarine had great valuables from Germany because it was heading away from Germany even though the war ended.

"I think the rumour developed because U-3523 was a very modern, long-distance U-boat and some Nazis tried to escape with valuables in the last days.

"But the submarine was going to Norway, and not to South America with Nazis and valuables."

Much of the conspiracy theory involving Hitler's alleged escape have been propped up by the release of US intelligence documents that were declassified. A particular document of concern involved a claim that Hitler had been spotted by a witness in Argentina roughly a month following the British attack on the German submarine.

"By pre-arranged plan with six top Argentine officials, pack horses were waiting for the group and by daylight, all supplies were loaded on the horses and an all-day trip inland toward the foothills of the southern Andes was started," the document read, churning up years of conspiracy theories.

CHAPTER THIRTY-FOUR

HITLER: 'SECOND COMING OF JESUS CHRIST'

The article, Christ on the Crooked Cross: The Divinity of Jesus in Hitler's *Weltanschauung* by Mikael Nilsson (Published in Journal of Religious History, May 2021) argues that Hitler not only considered Jesus to be an example for every National Socialist but that he also considered him divine. Previous scholarship has shown that Hitler was a firm believer in God and that he did have a positive view of Jesus even though he expressed only contempt for the Christianity of the established churches.

Hitler was even convinced that he was the Messiah and openly admitted fantasising about himself as Jesus Christ, secret CIA files reveal. Declassified documents reveal the Nazi leader was nurturing dreams of being the second coming in his formative years before becoming the Fuhrer.

Hitler was labelled as having a "Messiah Complex" in a secret 68-page personality profile compiled by US spies in 1942. Intelligence files marked "top secret" by the Office of Strategic Services (OSS) -a forerunner to the CIA were described as a "biographical sketch" of the Hitler for Washington. The documents were penned almost exactly one year after the US joined World War II. It has an entire section detailing Hitler's so-called Messiah

Complex and includes an anecdote in which Hitler told pals he imagined being Jesus.

CHAPTER THIRTY-FIVE

DID CHRIST ESCAPE TO KASHMIR?

Nikolai AleksandrovichaliasNotovitch was a CrimeanJewish adventurer and reporter, known for his 1894 book claiming that during the unknown years of Jesus, he left Galilee for India and studied with Hindus and Buddhists before returning to Judea.

Notovitch's claim was based on a document he said he had seen at the Hemis Monastery while he stayed there. The consensus view amongst modern scholars is that Notovitch's account of the travels of Jesus to India was a hoax.

After breaking his leg in India and while recovering from it at the Hemis monastery in Ladakh, Notovitch learned of the Tibetan manuscript *Life of Saint Issa, Best of the Sons of Men* -Isa being the Arabic name of Jesus in Islam. Notovitch's account, with the text of the *Life*, was published in French in 1894 as *La vie inconnue de Jésus-Christ*. It was translated into English, German, Spanish, and Italian.

Notovitch's book generated controversy as soon as it was published. The philologist Max Müller expressed incredulity at the account presented and suggested that either Notovitch was the victim of a practical joke or he had fabricated the evidence. Müller wrote: "Taking it for granted that M. Notovitch is a gentleman and not a liar, we cannot help thinking that the Buddhist monks of Ladakh and Tibet must be wags, who enjoy mystifying inquisitive travelers, and that M. Notovitch fell far too easy a victim to their jokes. "Müller then wrote to the head lama at Hemis monastery to ask about the document and Notovitch's story. The head lama replied that there had been no western visitor at the monastery in the previous fifteen years, during which he had been the head lama there, and there were no documents related to Notovitch's story.

But Fida Hassnain, a Kashmiri writer, has stated: Notovitch responded publicly by announcing his existence, along with the names of people he met on his travels in Kashmir and Ladakh. He also offered to return to Tibet in the company of recognized orientalists to verify the authenticity of the verses contained in his compilation. In the French journal *La Paix*, he affirmed his belief in the Orthodox Church and advised his detractors to restrict themselves to the simple issue of the existence of the Buddhist scrolls at Hemis.

Swami Abhedananda (1866-1939) was a disciple of Sri Ramakrishna Paramhansa Deva. The Swami went to the USA in 1897, when Swami Vivekananda asked him to take charge of the Vedanta Society in New York, where he preached messages of Vedanta and teachings of his Guru for about 25 years, travelling far and wide to the United States, Canada, Mexico, Japan, and Hong Kong.

While living in North America, he made the acquaintance of people like Thomas Edison, William James, and Dr. Max Muller. He was initially skeptical of Notovitch's claims. Finally, he returned to India in 1921. In 1922, he travelled through Kashmir and Tibet. It was a long and strenuous journey at that time across a difficult terrain from the plains of India to snow-capped Tibet. He visited the Hemis monastery whilst verifying the reports of Notovich that he had heard the previous year in the U.S. He claimed that lamas at the monastery confirmed to him that Notovich was brought to the monastery with a broken leg and he was nursed there for a month and a half. They also told him that the Tibetan manuscript on Issa was shown to Notovich and its contents interpreted so that he could translate them into Russian. This manuscript was shown to Swami Abhedananda, which had 14 chapters, containing

223 couplets (slokas). He had some portions of the manuscript translated with the help of a lama, about 40 verses of which appeared in Swami's travelogue. The original Pali manuscript -allegedly composed after Christ's resurrection was said to be in the monastery of Marbour near Lhasa.

The old manuscript that they showed Swami Abhedananda says that Christ moved to India at 13, partially to escape his parents and keep them from forcing him to marry. During Christ's travels in India, he learned how to read and understand the Vedas. He later spent 6 years with Buddhists and learned Pali and studied all the Buddhist scriptures. The swami further says, "The lama said that after the resurrection, Jesus Christ came secretly to Kashmir and lived in a monastery surrounded by many disciples."

After his return to Bengal, the Swami asked his assistant Bhairab Chaitanya to prepare a manuscript of the travelogue based on the notes he had taken. The manuscript was published serially in *Visvavani*, a monthly publication of the Ramakrishna Vedanta Samiti, in 1927 and subsequently published in a book form in Bengali. The fifth edition of the book in English was published in 1987, which also contains an English translation of Notovich's *Life of Saint Issa* as an appendix.

Nicholas Roerich was a Russian painter, writer, archaeologist, theosophist, perceived by some in Russia as an enlightener, philosopher who in his youth was influenced by a movement in Russian society around the spiritual. Paramahansa Yogananda wrote that Nicholas Roerich also supported Notovich's and Swami Abhedananda's story during his visit to Tibet in the mid-1920s. He also wrote that "records of Jesus's years in India were preserved in Puri, according to Bharati Krishna Tirtha, and that after leaving Puri Jesus spent "six years with the Sakya Buddhist sect in Nepal and Tibet", before returning to Palestine. He added that "the overall value of these records is inestimable in a search for the historical Jesus".

Mirza Ghulam Ahmad, the founder of the Ahmadiyya movement in Islam, wrote *Jesus in India* (published in 1908) and claimed that

Jesus had traveled to India after surviving his crucifixion, but specifically disagreed with Notovitch that Jesus had gone to India before then.

Ahmadiyya Islam considers Jesus as a human mortal man and a prophet of God, born to the virgin Mary. Jesus is understood to have survived the crucifixion based on the account of the canonical Gospels, the Quran, the hadith, and revelations (*ilham* and *kashaf*) to Mirza Ghulam Ahmad. Having delivered his message to the Israelites in Judea, Jesus is understood to have emigrated eastward to escape persecution from Judea and to have further spread his message to the Lost Tribes of Israel. In Ahmadiyya Islam, Jesus is thought to have died a natural death in India. Jesus lived to old age and later died in Srinagar, Kashmir, and his tomb is presently located at the "Rozabal" shrine.

In his book '*Jesus Lived in India*', German author Holger Kersten also promoted the ideas of Nicolas Notovich and Mirza Ghulam Ahmad of Qadian.

CHAPTER THIRTY-SIX

Führer's Connection with the Maharajas

Hitler considered the Indians to be racially inferior and unfit. He had no desire whatsoever to meet any Indian leader, especially a leader who was pushing the case for Indian independence but Bose was a pragmatist and a realist. He just wanted assistance against the British, he had absolutely no love for Hitler. In his meeting with Hitler on May 29 in 1942, despite being given very little room to speak, Bose still brought up the issue of the anti-India remarks in Mein Kampf, requesting that Hitler clarify Germany's attitude towards India. It was only Bose, who could tell Adolf Hitler on the face to correct his autobiography. Not even the colossal megalomaniac dictator could swerve Bose's love for India. Bose's pursuit of the issue of Hitler's denunciations shows his sense of integrity and commitment to this country.

For Bose, things in Germany didn't work out the way he intended them to, despite his best efforts. Bose planned to go to Japan, and attack British India with Japan's help. Hitler arranged a U-180 German submarine for Bose. On 8th/9th February 1943, the submarine sailed from Keil. But as to what transpired in the meeting between Hitler and Bose, we don't know a lot. The absence of information also leads to people projecting different theories.

Bose in the top Congress hierarchy before his exit:
Reported in the The New Indian Express on 24th January, 2022: In many ways, 1938 and 1939 were the moment of truth in a large number of Indian Princely States as powerful people's movements flourished against the high handedness of the Ruling dispensation which directly drew its strength from the Paramount Power in the Princely States.

The challenge to the troika of Gandhiji, Nehru and Patel also came around the same time. At the Haripura Congress, Subhas Chandra Bose became president of the Congress and a year later in Tripuri, he forced the issue again despite strident opposition from the trio and won the Presidency by 95 votes more than Gandhiji's candidate Pattabhi Sitaramayya. After Bose won convincingly, Gandhi said Pattabhi's defeat was "more mine than his". At Tripuri in March 1939, GB Pant moved a resolution asking Bose to appoint a Working Committee in line with Gandhi's ideas. Bose in a passionate presidential address on March 10, 1939, where very specifically focusing on the Princely States, his opinion coalesced with Nehru, stated, "But since Haripura much has happened. Today we find that the Paramount Power is in league with the State authorities in most places. In such circumstances, should we of the Congress not draw closer to the people of the States? I have no doubt in my own mind as to what our duty is today. Besides lifting the above ban, the work of guiding the popular movements in the States for Civil Liberty and Responsible Government should be conducted by the Working Committee on a comprehensive and systematic basis. The work so far done has been of a piecemeal nature and there has hardly been any system or plan behind it. But the time has come when the Working Committee should assume this responsibility and discharge it in a comprehensive and systematic way and, if necessary, appoint a special sub-committee for the purpose."

The tricky relationship between the closed group controlled by Gandhiji in the Congress Working Committee those days was patently unhappy with the entry of a powerful and popular outsider in Bose.

Though Nehru privately and often publicly remained for most part on Bose's right side in this tussle. This proxy war resulted in Bose leaving the Congress and taking up the path of freeing India from the yoke of British rule by raising an army through a war time collaboration with the help of Axis powers.

The Princely States and the Hindu Imaginary:

In his article, *Princely States and the Hindu Imaginary: Exploring the Cartography of Hindu Nationalism in Colonial India* (The Journal of Asian Studies Vol. 67, No. 3, August 2008), Manu Bhagavan explores that though the Hindu Mahasabha and the Rashtriya Swayamsevak Sangh (RSS) became sibling organizations, it was the Mahasabha which came to the forefront of the Hindu nationalist movement as a whole. There were two primary vehicles through which they spread their message. First of these was a newspaper called *Hindu Outlook* (hereafter *HOK*), the official mouthpiece of the Hindu Mahasabha. The second medium consisted of conferences and regional meetings at which speeches were made by Mahasabha leaders.

Comparing Hitler to God and con-joining the unification of Germany with that of India, Bhai Parmanand, a leader of the Hindu Mahasabha, wrote in 1938, "He is Hitler .... The message that he sent on the annexation in which he described himself as a tool in the hands of the Lord of Destiny for the unification of Germany reminded me of the assurance of Lord Krishna that whenever the world has need of him, He manifests himself.... Is the unity of India complete? I submit not" (*HOK*, April 27, 1938,3). He declared, "Make this address your Mein Kampf.... Make Savarkar your Fehurer [sic]" (*HOK*, January 11, 1939,1).

Bhagavan writes, as early as the late 1930s, princely states featured prominently in *HOK*. But as the 1940s dawned and progressed, as both independence and a possible partition began to gain traction as realistic near-future possibilities, the Mahasabha directed ever-greater attention to these regions. In April 1944, the Mahasabha organized three major conferences to address the place of princely states in their idea of India, all held, not coincidentally, in the princely realms of Mysore and Baroda, territories. Not incidentally, *HOK* devoted an entire page to an obituary for Sayaji Rao when he passed away.

Bhagavan continues, the Maharaja of Baroda Pratapsingh Rao Gaekwad, grandson of Sayaji Rao Gaekwad III, had only acceded to the throne in 1939 following his grandfather's death. Indeed, some of the major princes in power in the 1940s, including those of Mysore (Jayachamaraja Wadiyar, acceded 1940) and Bikaner (Sadul Singh Rathor, acceded 1943), had only come to power recently. Their legitimacy and overall hold on authority were therefore much more tentative. Various princes in the 1940s may have latched onto Hindutva as one of the only viable means to maintain their status, especially considering the failure to gain traction of the idea of "postcolonial federation."

From 1938 until 1947, writers in *HOK*, the main intellectual forum for the organization, paid consistent attention to the princely states of Baroda, Gwalior, Hyderabad, Kashmir Mysore, and Travancore.

There are surprising revelations about Fuhrer's connections to the Maharajas of princely states in India under British rule just before WW II.

Bhupinder Singh, Maharaja of Patiala:
Maharaja Bhupinder Singh was the king of the princely state of Patiala in the North of India. With fertile lands of Punjab under his province, the king had immense wealth at his disposal. Maharaja Bhupinder Singh was known for his rich interest in jewels and costly materials. Maharaja owned more than 27 Rolls Royces, The Maharaja was also famous for his tour around the world. He befriended monarchs in Europe on his trips.

In the book *The Automobiles of the Maharajas* by Sharda Dwivedi, Raja Malvinder Singh, the grandson of Maharaja Bhupinder Singh recounted. "My grandfather Maharaja Bhupinder Singh went to Germany in 1935 and asked to see Adolf Hitler who very reluctantly gave him 10 to 15 minutes. They got into conversation, one thing led to another and 15 minutes became 30 and then 60. The Fuhrer asked grandfather to stay on for lunch and then asked him to come back the next day and then the third day. On the third day, he gave him German weapons like Lignose, Walther, and Luger pistols and a magnificent Maybach.

The only two other rulers who were gifted cars by Hitler were King Farouk of Egypt and the Joddha Shamsher Rana of Nepal. It is believed that Hitler wanted to enhance his friendship with the Maharaja, so the princely state of Patiala might take a neutral stand in case of a war between Germany and Britain.

There were only six cars of this type ever made. The car was shipped to India and got a place in the Maharaja's garage. The vehicle was hidden from plain sight after the start of World War II and never used. After the war, the Maybach with Maharaja was probably the only model in the world that survived. The Maharaja gave the car as a gift to one of these friends, who later sold it to an American buyer. In 2015 the car came for an auction in Amsterdam and sold to an anonymous buyer for an undisclosed amount. The story emphasizes the interwar period in the 1930s, where friendship and alliance made and broke in months. The car was a symbol of diplomacy to cause a crack in the jewel of the British crown -India.

Sayajirao Gaekwad, Maharaja of Baroda:

It was reported in Times of India on Aug 15, 2010: According to a new Marathi book that will hit the stands in September, ruler of erstwhile Baroda state, Sayajirao Gaekwad, met the German dictator during the 1936 Berlin Olympics for India's freedom.

Gaekwad even signed a secret pact with Hitler to get his support for India's freedom. It was known as the Baroda-Berlin Pact. Gaekwad's personal assistant Vishnu Nene was sent to Germany to arrange the meeting. "Gaekwad believed an enemy's enemy is a friend. So, he decided to join hands with Hitler," says Dr Damodar Nene, who has written a new biography of Gaekwad and gives details of the pact. He is Vishnu Nene's son. The book, 'Sayajirao Gaekwad Chi Biography' has been published by Ved Gandharva publishers of Pune.

To ensure that the British don't suspect anything, Gaekwad took their permission to attend the Berlin Olympics. "His box was placed right under Hitler's during the opening ceremony," Nene says. Gaekwad is believed to have promised Hitler the support of all Hindu princes in case of a war in Europe. "It was agreed that Hindu princes would back Hitler during the World War II and Hitler would support India in its freedom struggle. The pact was kept a well-guarded secret as the British would have considered it an act of treason," adds Nene.

"Gaekwad signed the pact as chancellor of the Chamber of Princes and was confident that all the members would support him," Nene says. The chamber was established in 1920 by royal proclamation to provide a forum to rulers of the princely states to voice their concerns to the British. It survived until 1947. As reported, the pact was forgotten after Gaekwad died in 1939 even as the world stood on the brink of a devastating war.

CHAPTER THIRTY-SEVEN

COULD HITLER BE BURIED IN KASHMIR?

Using never seen before FBI documents, ex-UN war crimes investigator John Cencich Kand journalist Gerrard Williams concluded Hitler escaped the fall of the Third Reich in 1945. Following an investigation, they found Hitler slipped away from Berlin moments before the Soviets invaded -making his way to the Canary Islands and then South America.

But now a conspiracy theory suggests the Nazi dictator may have actually taken sanctuary after the war in remote Kashmir in India which was then a British colony.

What is more extraordinary is that Hitler, who despised all forms of religion in favour of his warped death cult -might be buried in a shrine reputed to be Jesus Christ's final resting place.

Patrick Knox reports in Daily Star, UK: The theory that Hitler fled to Kashmir via the Middle East and Afghanistan has been floating around among Kashmiris for years. But it has only gained traction after the investigation by Mr. Cencich and Mr. Williams concluded Hitler escaped the fall of the Third Reich alive.

Spearheading the theory is respected Kashmiri writer and historian Farooq Renzu Shah. He insists: "Hitler escaped to Kashmir, India, where his grave is in Rozbal garden" It is speculated that during Maharaja Hari Singh's time one mysterious personality arrived secretly. The only Maharaja who was close to him through Subash Chandra Bose was Hari Singh.

Therefore, there is more probability that the mysterious personality who was given shelter in the secret place of "Rozabal" was the same.

Mr. Shah says, "The grave of Hitler was titled in the name of Yasuh (Jesus) in Rozabal and rumours were spread that the grave is of Jesus to keep it highly guarded secret to conceal fact about it actually is grave of Hitler,"

In the shabby backstreets of Srinagar is an old building known as the Rozabal shrine. But it is padlocked tight, and it has a watchman guarding it to make sure no one goes near the corpse.

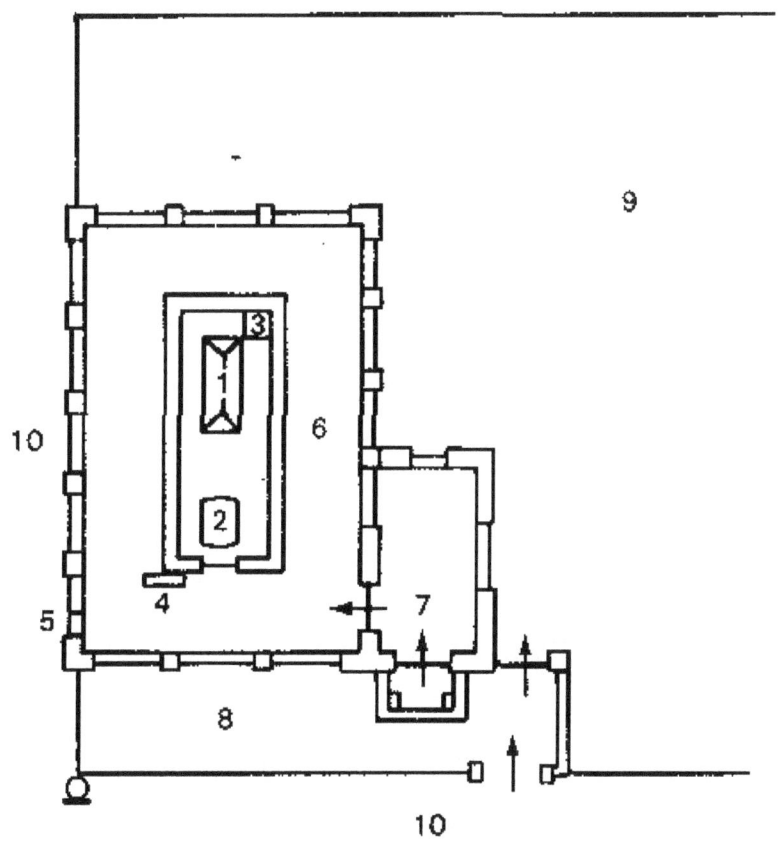

Plan of the "Rozabal", the "tomb of Yuz Asaf (Jesus*)" [Source: *Jesus died in Kashmir* by Andreas Faber Kaiser]

1. Tombstone of Yuza Asaf (Jesus?)
2. Tombstone of Syed Nasir-ud-Din
3. Carved footprints
4. Explanatory tables
5. Access to crypt (now blocked, except for a small window)
6. Gallery
7. Entrance hall

8. Palio
9. Moslem cemetery
10. Street
11. Post with the "Rozabal" notica

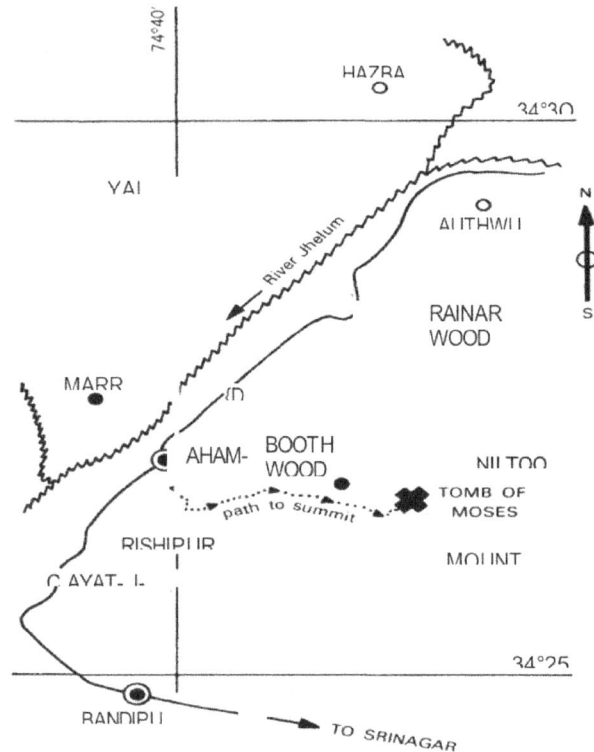

Map showing the "tomb of Moses" and surrounding area
[Source: *Jesus died in Kashmir* by Andreas Faber Kaiser]

Mr. Shah believes the truth about Hitler could be found in official documents which he is now calling to be declassified. He claims Adolf was pals with Indian nationalist, Netaji Subhas Chandra Bose. Bose collaborated with the Japanese in the fight against British rule in India. Bose headed the Indian National Army -devoted to booting out the Brits. He even lived in Third Reich for a spell during the war. Using his connections in India, he was said to have arranged a safe haven for the Nazi chief among the then Maharaja of Kashmir who kept the world's most hated man in his palace, lavishing him in a life of luxury amid stunning scenery. He believes that it was Subhas Chandra Bose's INA, which helped Hitler reach Kashmir where he breathed his last.

Is there any possible link between the arguments of Prof. Nandalal Chakrabarti that the ex-INA men tried to facilitate their leader's safe passage to Kashmir by leading the tribesmen to the Valley to establish a completely free zone there and what Kashmiri writer and historian Farooq Renzu Shah believes that INAhelped Hitler reach Kashmir -the believed Aryan Valley or the place where Jesus Christ breathed his last?

Andreas Faber Kaiser also described in *Jesus Died in Kashmir: Jesus, Moses and the 10 Lost Tribes of Israel* (English translation by Gordon Cremonesi Ltd 1977,16-18) about the manuscript transcribed by Notovich that Jesus came to Jagannath in Orissa, where the remains of Vyasa-Krishna were. There the priests of Brahma taught him to read and understand the Vedas. Jesus lived six years in Jagannath, Rajagriha, Benares, and other holy cities before leaving for the Himalayas.

Ahmadiyya writer Khwaja Nazir Ahmad also claimed in *Jesus in Heaven and Earth* (1952) that Jesus (identified with Yuz Asaf), Thomas the Apostle (held to be Jesus' twin brother), and their mother Mary travelled to India, with Mary dying en route from Taxila at Muree and being buried at Pindi Point there, later named "Mai Mari da Ashtan".

Kashmir O Tibbote Swami Abhedananda (Third Edition, 1955, 145–148), describes Jesus's relationship with the Nath community. Notes are given that the tomb of Jesus Christ is still located in Khanyar.

The "Rozabal" shrine is located in the Khanyar quarter in the downtown area of Srinagar in Kashmir.

During his visit to the Hemis monastery, Swami Abhedananda came to know that the former Maharaja of Kashmir, Pratap Singh, had paid Rs. 30,000 for the renovation work of the Mohantaji of this monastery sided with the Maharaja and promised to provide six months of food and shelter to all his troops. That is why this monastery has always been associated with the Kashmir Maharajas.

Kashmir O Tibbote Swami Abhedananda reveals that the revered Swami Akhandananda Maharaj, a disciple of Sri Ramakrishna Paramhansa, visited the monastery from Baranagar Math in 1888.

Oi Mahamanab Ase (Jayasree Prakashan -a sister organisation of Jayasree Patrika, a monthly magazine which was founded by Leela Roy (Nee Leelabati Nag) -a front-ranking revolutionary, a patriot of legendary fame, and a close associate of Netaji Subhas Chandra Bose. Jayasree Prakashan started its journey in the early sixties of the last century.) is a collection of his vision, plan of action, spiritual and political advice, minute details of national and international political incidents that the renunciate Bengali monk 'Gumnamibaba' alias 'Bhagwanji' or 'Mahakaal' narrated to his diehard Bengal followers in course of his numerous meetings with them. The book includes articles, letters, and reports having links with Bose's life after death -mostly narrated in a cryptic language and presented as a riddle under the pen name *Charanik* because of the strict injunction of Bhagwanji himself. Obeying his order, his disciples never discussed their interactions with their leader in public. They never regarded the holy man who stayed at Naimisharanya-Neemsar, and various other places in Uttar Pradesh as anyone other than Netaji Subhas Chandra Bose.

Bhagwanji categorically told his close Bengali followers about Jesus Christ, was initially published in *Jayashree Patrika* in May 1974, and later included in *Oi Mahamanab Ase, Akhaṇḍa sanskaraṇa*, 176, 440 (loosely translated from Bengali): "Jesus belonged to the Nath community. The Atharva Veda and the Hindu scriptures were used to prepare Jesus's dictums. Jesus's Guru had instructed him to preach the religion outside of India. Jesus was accompanied by John. Isha and Mother Marian are both in this country. They are still there. I am alive, and I will prove it by revealing all of these events and creations one by one."

"Three very old gypsies told me, 'The lost tribes' of 'Jesus' are not lost. They just got married in another place. They gave directions to the road, but I could not go- due to my 'Mission.' These are the ones who informed me conclusively who Jesus got as a Sadguru from the Nathyogi community of India, who had a deep connection with Bengal."

Based on the report of Professor Atul Sen searching for Netaji Subhas Chandra Bose, where he was said to be living like a saint in seclusion, Dr. Pabitra Mohan Roy -INA's Secret Service Officer went to Naimisharanya (Neemsar) in Uttar Pradesh towards the end of 1962. He was able to finally meet the saint in a dilapidated temple in Naimisharanya. After having spoken to him he was convinced that the sanyasi was none other than Netaji Subhas Chandra Bose.

Dr. Pabitra Mohan confided everything to the revolutionary Leela Roy. Leela Roy went to Naimishranya in March 1963, accompanied by Kaviraj Kamalakanta Ghosh, Shaila Sen, Prof Samar Guha, & Anil Das of INA Secret Service. After her contact with Bhagwanji was established, she deputed her trusted revolutionary, Kaviraj Kamalakanta Ghosh to serve medical attention to her leader.

After the death of Kamalakanta Ghosh, *Charanik* discovered some small pieces of papers having notes and interactions between Bhagwanji and Kamalakanta (Published in *Jayashree Patrika* in August 1974, and later included in *Oi Mahamanab Ase*, 178). At one place Bhagwanji's narrations about his secretive nature concealing personal emotions are noted by *Charanik*, where, there is a cryptical question asked by him:

"SHIMLER" ... Could you ever know his mind?

Did he want to give a clue about any secret of the leader of the SS Heinrich Himmler or Hitler?

We further come to know about Bhagwanji's narratives on fascism -as noted by *Charanik* (first published in *Jayashree Patrika* in August 2013 and recently in *Oi Mahamanab Ase, Asesa sanskaraṇa*, 2022, 101-102).

Bhagwanji narrates, "During the Indo-Pak war of 1965, the biggest Sanghchalaks of the RSS worked in the very active field of the front line. Not in hundreds but in millions."

"...This is funny that the first thing is from the outside -everyone says, dictatorial fascists. To them, indiscipline is democracy. They do not know what fascism is, how devilish fascism is."

In 1965, the Indian subcontinent was going through a turbulent time due to an all-out war with Pakistan. The severity of the seventeen-day war was the largest engagement of armoured vehicles and the largest tank battle since World War II. After Pakistani forces attempted to infiltrate the Indian part of Kashmir, Prime Minister Lal Bahadur Shastri retaliated by launching a military assault against the infiltration.

At a time when our country was at war, Lal Bahadur Shastri decided to cut across party lines and invited RSS Sarsanghchalak (Chief) Shri Guruji MS Golwalkar, to an All-Party Meet.

The purpose of the invitation was to task the Delhi Police with more strategic activities and relieve them of their routine duties which were then taken over by RSS workers, says Dr. Harish Chandra Barthwal in his book, *The Rashtriya Swayamsewak Sangh: An Introduction*. Barthwal even goes further to claim that upon Shastri's request, RSS workers also provided food and other essential supplies to soldiers deployed on the war front.

CHAPTER THIRTY-EIGHT

Declassified FBI Document

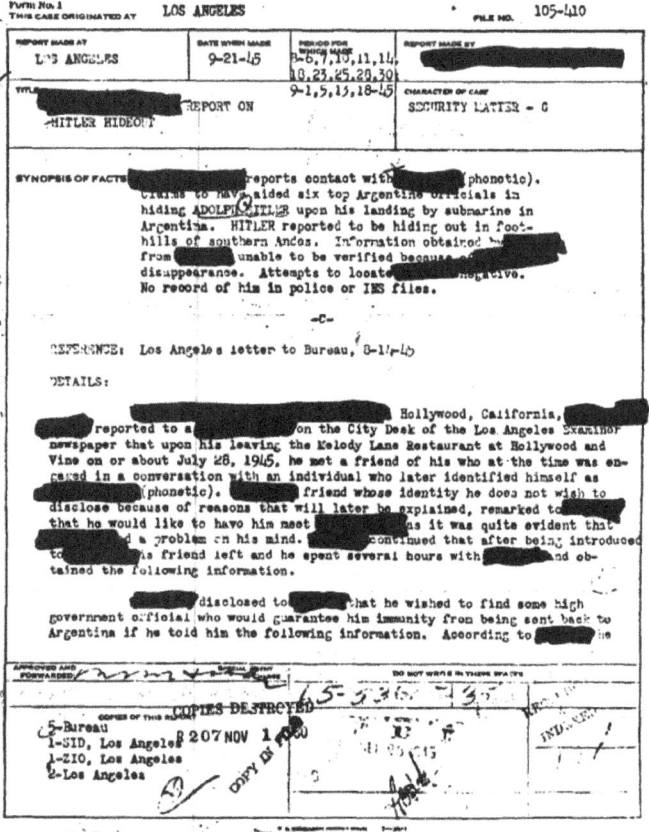

105-410

was one of four men who met HITLER and his party when they landed from two submarines in Argentina approximately two and one-half weeks after the fall of Berlin. ▆▆▆ continued that the first sub came close to shore about 11:00 p.m. after it had been signaled that it was safe to land and a doctor and several men disembarked. Approximately two hours later the second sub came ashore and HITLER, two women, another doctor, and several more men, making the whole party arriving by submarines approximately 50, were aboard. By pre-arranged plan with six top Argentine officials, pack horses were waiting for the group and by daylight all supplies were loaded on the horses and an all-day trip inland toward the foothills of the southern Andes was started. At dusk the party arrived at the ranch where HITLER and his party, according to ▆▆▆, are now in hiding. ▆▆▆ most specifically explained that the subs landed along the tip of the Valdez Peninsula along the southern tip of Argentina in the gulf of San Matias. ▆▆▆ told ▆▆▆ that there are several tiny villages in this area where members of HITLER's party would eventually stay with German families. He named the towns as San Antonio, Videma, Neuquen, Muster, Carmena, and Rason.

▆▆▆ maintains that he can name the six Argentine officials and also the names of the three other men who helped HITLER inland to his hiding place. ▆▆▆ explained that he was given $15,000 for helping in the deal. ▆▆▆ explained to ▆▆▆ that he was hiding out in the United States now so that he could later tell how he got out of Argentina. He stated to ▆▆▆ that he would tell his story to the United States officials after HITLER's capture so that they might keep him from having to return to Argentina. He further explained to ▆▆▆ that the matter was weighing on his mind and that he did not wish to be mixed up in the business any further.

According to ▆▆▆, HITLER is suffering from asthma and ulcers, has shaved off his mustache and has a long "but" on his upper lip.

▆▆▆ gave the following directions to ▆▆▆ "If you will go to a hotel in San Antonio, Argentina, I will arrange for a man to meet you there and locate the ranch where HITLER is. It is heavily guarded, of course, and you will be risking your life to go there. If you do go to Argentina, place an ad in the Examiner stating, ▆▆▆ call Hempstead 8458,' and I know that you are on the way to San Antonio."

The above information was given to ▆▆▆, reporter on the Los Angeles Examiner on July 29, 1945.

The writer contacted ▆▆▆ in an attempt to locate ▆▆▆ in order that he might be vigorously interviewed in detail concerning the above store. ▆▆▆ reiterated the information set out above, adding that the friend to whom ▆▆▆ was talking in front of the Melody Lane Restaurant was a friend of his by the name of "JACK," last name unknown, but that since the introduction he has had further conversation with "JACK" and "JACK" advised him that while he was eating his lunch at the Melody Lane Restaurant ▆▆▆ sat at his table

-2-

LA 105-410

and after the meal followed him out where he engaged in a conversation in front of the restaurant. ▓▓▓ according to "JACK," had mentioned that he had important information to divulge and solicited his cooperation in locating the proper officials to whom to impart this information. "JACK" told ▓▓▓ that it was at this time that ▓▓▓ came along and he asked ▓▓▓ to listen to his story inasmuch as he, "JACK," was in a hurry.

▓▓▓ added that he had spent several hours engaged in general conversation which he explained was a "feeler" on the part of ▓▓▓ to determine if he, ▓▓▓ was all right and could be relied upon. He then advanced the story which has been related above.

▓▓▓ advised that he told ▓▓▓ he would try to help him, and for him to call back at the Hempstead number in a few days and he would have some information for him. ▓▓▓ continued that he immediately contacted ▓▓▓ at the Examiner and ▓▓▓ tried to arrange a meeting with ▓▓▓ and in the meantime inserted the story in the newspaper which, according to ▓▓▓ evidently scared ▓▓▓ stated that he was unable to throw any more light on the story inasmuch as all the information obtained from ▓▓▓ is incorporated in the story. ▓▓▓ according to ▓▓▓, did not spell his name but simply introduced himself as ▓▓▓ which is phonetic.

▓▓▓ was advised by the writer that if ▓▓▓ telephoned him or if he was observed at any time to immediately engage him in conversation to explain that the proper authorities wished to discuss the matter further in detail with him personally. To date ▓▓▓ has not contacted ▓▓▓.

▓▓▓ advised that he eats two meals daily at the Melody Lane Restaurant but he has not observed the subject since his first meeting. The writer has continually spot-checked the Melody Lane Restaurant at meal time in an effort to locate ▓▓▓ with negative results.

The Hollywood and Los Angeles police records have been checked with negative results on the name ▓▓▓ and other similar sounding names.

The records of Immigration and Naturalization Service were also checked with negative results under the name ▓▓▓ and similar sounding names with negative results.

Because of the lack of sufficient information to support the story advanced by ▓▓▓, it is believed impossible to continue efforts to locate HITLER with the sparse information obtained to date.

▓▓▓ tells an apparently reliable story but admits there is some doubt in his mind as to whether ▓▓▓ is telling the truth.

A description of ▓▓▓ obtained from ▓▓▓ is as follows:

-3-

> Dear Sir:
> I'll bet a dollar to a doughnut that Hitler, is located right in New York city!
> There's no other city in the world where he could so easily be absorbed. No doubt you have considered this possibility, but I mention it for what it is worth anyway.

Mr. J. Edgar Hoover.
Chief of Bureau of Natl Investigators.
Washington D. C.

My dear Mr. Hoover:

For quite long weeks I have been planning to write to you but due to excess of work I could not. That delay has come very a propos, as in the meantime it has been offered a reward to anyone whose information may conduct to the detection of Hitler.

To begin with, I am one of those who think and believe firmily that Adolf Hitler as well as Eva Braun are alive. Their bodies have not been found, both vanished at the same time, both were not capable of committing suicide and with plenty of means, there is not a reason why they should not be as safe as possible, trying to enjoy life.

Now, as to the whereabouts my reasoning is this:

1- Hitler disappeared the very day before the Russians entered Berlin; there was no large margin of time for him to prepare his escapade.

2- Hitler did not learn any language -foreing one-, pretended to despise all languages, naturally besides the German, but the real reason must be, he tried and could not. So he must have thought of a country in which his German would not attract the attention of others.

3- Switzerland -tho denying it now-, played ball all the time during the war with the nazi Reich. The German Switzers are numerous and powerful, and, which is more important, they were, are, the nearest friends to whom rich Hitler could apply for shelter. Besides the German part of Switzerland is peopled with far cited and practically isolated farms, in any of which Hitler and the Braun woman could live peacefully and happily for the rest of their natural lives.

Consequently I have a hunch that it is in the German Switzerland where these fugitives of law are to be found. They must be there, covered and helped by many other Switzer of German descent, afiliated to the nazi ideas.

Wishing you all good luck in your tasks, let me remain,

Yours very sincerely,

FEC:FMC

October 26, 1945

Dear

I have received your letter of October 22, 1945, transmitting a clipping from the "Magazine Digest" for November, 1945, on the possibility that Adolf Hitler may be in Argentina.

Your action in transmitting this clipping to me is indeed appreciated.

Sincerely yours,

John Edgar Hoover
Director

Nov 13th 1945

Federal Bureau of Investigation
Dear Sirs,—

I have a book here of Adolf Hitler it is all actual photographs taken in Germany of him and his colleagues. its all printed in German, so far I have found no one who can translate it. I thought it might be of interest in finding or tracing down some of the War Criminals.

I would be glad if you would have some one call who could talk German, it is best to call of an evening. My son who was over Seas there, traded a package of cigarettes for it & he sent it to me. I received it the middle of July it was about 4 weeks coming. He sent it with several other things and it was censored.

I hope I can get in touch with some one who is interested in this book. there is 125 pages in it & about 300 pictures, Please let me hear from you

Date: November 13, 1945

To: Mr. ████████
The American Embassy
Buenos Aires, Argentina

From: John Edgar Hoover – Director, Federal Bureau of Investigation

Subject: Hitler Hideout in Argentina
Security Matter – G

The Bureau is in receipt of a report from the Strategic Services Unit of the War Department dated October 23, 1945 concerning the possibility of a "Hitler Hideout" in Argentina. This report is as follows:

"One Mrs. Eichhorn, reported to be a reputable member of Argentine society and the proprietor of the largest spa hotel in La Falda, Argentina, recently made the following observations:

"a. that even before the Nazi Party was founded she made available to Goebbels her entire bank account which, at the time, amounted approximately to thirty thousand marks, which money was to be used for propaganda purposes;

"b. that she and her family have been enthusiastic supporters of Adolf Hitler since the Nazi Party was founded;

"c. that this voluntary support of the Nazi Party was never forgotten by Hitler and that during the years after he came into power her friendship with Hitler became so close that she and members of her family lived with Hitler in the same hotel on the occasion of their annual visit to Germany;

"d. that if Hitler should at any time get into difficulty wherein it was necessary for him to find a safe retreat, he would find such safe retreat at her hotel (La Falda) where they had already made the necessary preparations."

This is being furnished only for your information and for the completion of your files.

NAZI ENVOY SAYS HITLER STILL ALIVE

PARIS, Oct. 7 (IP) — The newspaper Francesoir today quoted Otto Abetz, Germany's wartime Ambassador to France, as saying in an interview that Adolf Hitler "is certainly not dead."

The newspaper said Abetz added that Hitler "was not a coward—I believe one day he will return."

Abetz's arrest was announced yesterday by French zone headquarters. The former Ambassador was captured as he sought to slip from the French to the United States zone of occupation.

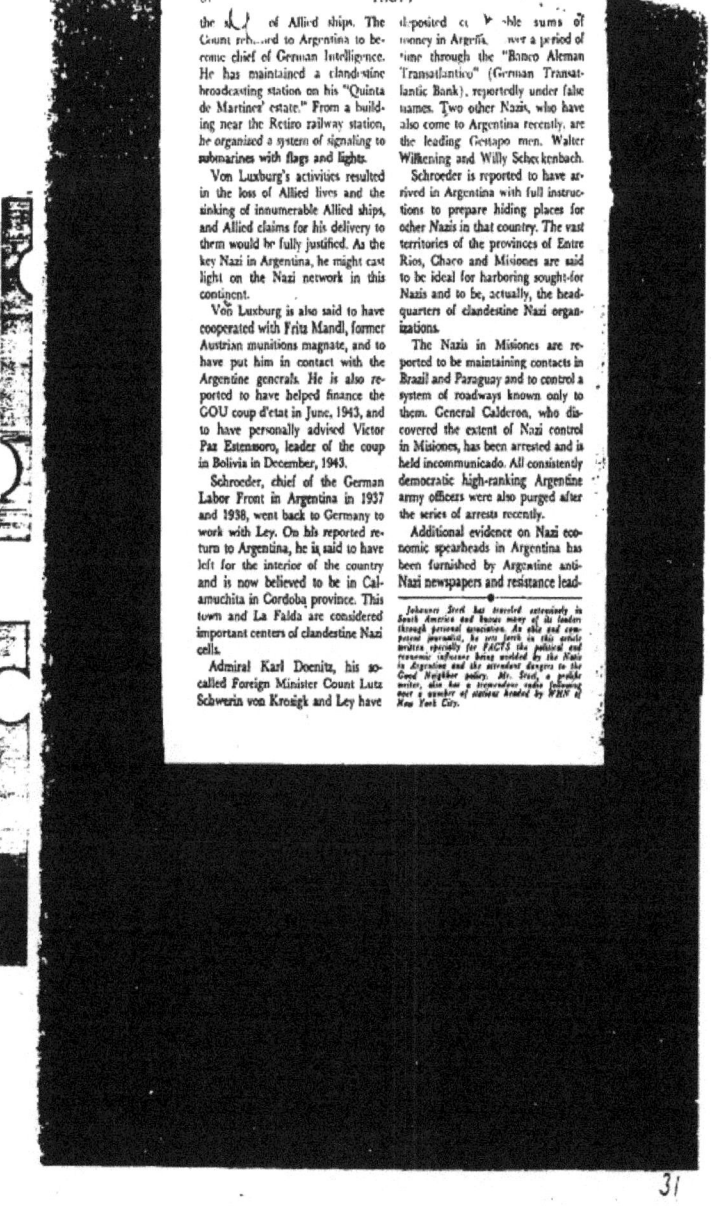

the s[...] of Allied ships. The Count ret[...]rd to Argentina to become chief of German Intelligence. He has maintained a clandestine broadcasting station on his "Quinta de Martinez' estate." From a building near the Retiro railway station, he organized a system of signaling to submarines with flags and lights.

Von Luxburg's activities resulted in the loss of Allied lives and the sinking of innumerable Allied ships, and Allied claims for his delivery to them would be fully justified. As the key Nazi in Argentina, he might cast light on the Nazi network in this continent.

Von Luxburg is also said to have cooperated with Fritz Mandl, former Austrian munitions magnate, and to have put him in contact with the Argentine generals. He is also reported to have helped finance the GOU coup d'etat in June, 1943, and to have personally advised Victor Paz Estenssoro, leader of the coup in Bolivia in December, 1943.

Schroeder, chief of the German Labor Front in Argentina in 1937 and 1938, went back to Germany to work with Ley. On his reported return to Argentina, he is said to have left for the interior of the country and is now believed to be in Calamuchita in Cordoba province. This town and La Falda are considered important centers of clandestine Nazi cells.

Admiral Karl Doenitz, his so-called Foreign Minister Count Lutz Schwerin von Krosigk and Ley have deposited c[...] able sums of money in Argentina over a period of time through the "Banco Aleman Transatlantico" (German Transatlantic Bank), reportedly under false names. Two other Nazis, who have also come to Argentina recently, are the leading Gestapo men, Walter Wiffkening and Willy Scheckenbach.

Schroeder is reported to have arrived in Argentina with full instructions to prepare hiding places for other Nazis in that country. The vast territories of the provinces of Entre Rios, Chaco and Misiones are said to be ideal for harboring sought-for Nazis and to be, actually, the headquarters of clandestine Nazi organizations.

The Nazis in Misiones are reported to be maintaining contacts in Brazil and Paraguay and to control a system of roadways known only to them. General Calderon, who discovered the extent of Nazi control in Misiones, has been arrested and is held incommunicado. All consistently democratic high-ranking Argentine army officers were also purged after the series of arrests recently.

Additional evidence on Nazi economic spearheads in Argentina has been furnished by Argentine anti-Nazi newspapers and resistance lead-

Johannes Steel has traveled extensively in South America and knows many of its leaders through personal association. As able and competent journalist, he sets forth in this article written specially for FACTS the political and economic influence being wielded by the Nazis in Argentina and the attendant dangers to the Good Neighbor policy. Mr. Steel, a prolific writer, also has a tremendous radio following over a number of stations headed by WHN of New York City.

why don't you go down to Pole Island and find Hitler ▓▓▓▓▓ owns the Island or his ▓▓▓ he Boildt - it is have his own to come to from Germany. he ▓▓ is dead but he has others to follow him. send the FBI and dont ask the Natives any Questions for they will not him wise for they are all fisherman.

I lived at ▓▓▓▓▓▓ 10 years and I know Mr + Mrs ▓▓▓▓ very well
it is was in 1920

50 JAN 8 - 1945

Hitler Mystery Deepens as Other Nazi Leaders Make Pleas to Live

By JOHN F. SEMBOWER
Written for Central Press and this Newspaper

THE HITLER mystery continues to grow daily. As most of the other Nazi bigwigs prepare to go on trial for their lives at Nuremberg, the most hunted of all the Nazis, Adolf Hitler, still is absent and unaccounted for.

Is Hitler dead or alive and in hiding? If he died, as most of his confederates claim, why has his body never been identified or found?

With each passing day the suspense mounts. If Hitler should be captured alive it would be one of the biggest stories of modern times. If he is never found and no trace of his remains is identified, he is almost certain to become the central figure of a legend.

In this last instance, the chances are that for years to come there will be persons all over the world who will report that they saw him alive after the fall of Berlin, that he got away and lived out his natural life.

Allied leaders dislike the prospect of this long drawn-out aftermath of the fall of Hitlerian Germany. Hitler's secretaries have told their captors that he was aware of what a final act of cunning it would be to disappear utterly. So far he has succeeded in doing this better than most things that he attempted in his hectic career.

Many Experts Dubious

Many of the world's greatest criminologists are on the hunt. They doubt the story of Hitler's chauffeur who contends that he burned the bodies of Hitler and his mistress, Eva Braun, with a can of gasoline in a shallow trench outside the chancellery. Famed Scotland Yard has pointed out that bodies are not nearly so easily obliterated.

Ninety-two charred and broken bodies were removed from a mass grave near Hitler's bunker in the Reichschancellary. They were subjected to much worse destruction than burning with gasoline, yet the remains were sufficiently identifiable to convince experts that none were those of Hitler and Eva Braun.

Criminologists have been busy building up one of the most complete descriptions ever compiled of a human being so that they will be able to make positive identification if likely remains are discovered.

They have painstakingly interviewed the dozen doctors who treated Hitler at one time or another, and have collected X-ray films of his teeth and such of his bones as were photographed. They have gone back into old police records of Hitler's arrests before he became chief of Germany on Jan. 30, 1933.

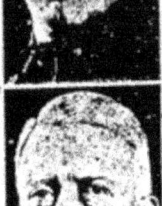

The searchers consider it more [...] in Germany itself.

If Hitler still lurks in Germany, sleuths believe that in time he will be "turned in" after the fashion that Foreign Minister Joachim von Ribbentrop was tattled on.

However, the greatest possibility for perpetuation of the Hitler mystery, whether he is dead or alive, lies in the very reports which already are being circulated.

Swedes report seeing an expensive yacht furtively moving in and out of countless inlets on the North sea. About the time that a Brazilian battleship was sunk by an unidentified submarine, a mysterious party, said to include a woman who might have been Eva Braun, was reported to have landed from a submarine off the coast of Argentina.

A Paris source reported that "Hitler is alive and dwelling in the Alto Adige region" of Italy. Mysterious goings and comings of large German-type transport planes in and out of mountainous regions of Spain have been told by some "observers."

A Japanese navy staff officer told details of a plan to evacuate Hitler and Eva Braun to Japan after the fall of Germany, and that a large Japanese submarine embarked on the enterprise.

Nothing further was heard of the submarine, according to the Jap. At the same time, some of the huge German U-boats still are unaccounted for.

Big Sub Cache

That there may have been considerable submarine traffic between Germany and Japan was indicated by the interception last July of a Nazi U-boat Japan-bound with a $5,000,000 cache of mercury and other valuables sorely needed by the Japs for a last-ditch stand.

Sufficient credence was attached to the possibility that high-ranking Germans might have escaped to Japan that United States Army authorities have been carefully checking the approximately three thousand Germans gathered in the remote mountain district of Antinopoyo, whose tall peaks resemble those of Hitler's beloved Bavaria.

Until and unless the Hitler mystery definitely is solved, these reports can continue and grow until they reach their ultimate end of someone reporting actually seeing Hitler himself in the flesh. Under much less tenuous circumstances, reports circulated for years that it was not Lincoln's assassin, John Wilkes Booth, who was shot to death by Union soldiers in a barn 12 days after the assassination, but a sleeping tramp who was mistaken for Booth.

Up until a few years ago it was necessary for official denial to be made that Booth did not evade justice and live out his natural life.

One of the greatest international [...] was that of the fabulous

ed Hitler at .... time or another, and have col..... X-ray films of his teeth and such at his bones as were photographed. They have gone back into old police records of Hitler's five arrests before he became chief of Germany on Jan. 30, 1933.

The searchers consider it more than an accident that no remains have been found which can be identified as those of Eva Braun or of Martin Bormann, deputy chief of the Nazi party, as well as Hitler.

Some German sources contend that Bormann superintended the cremation of Hitler and Eva Braun, and when last seen had Hitler's last testament naming him successor in the Nazi movement.

Bormann May Be Key

Allied authorities are inclined to believe that Bormann is the key to the mystery. If Hitler is alive, Bormann is likely to be with him, or to know his whereabouts.

If Hitler is dead, it is regarded as more plausible that the subtle Bormann engineered the complete disappearance of the bodies than that a chauffeur accomplished that result in the crude manner that he has described.

Among the flood of rumors is one to the effect that the Russians have Bormann in secret custody, and that they know the manner of Hitler's death, perhaps even possessing his corpse.

Allied authorities have attached no importance to the rumors, pointing out the irony that Hitler probably hoped that his disappearance might sow seeds of dissention among his conquerors.

There have been instances in history when the followers of dead leaders have tried to perpetuate their force through complete concealment of their remains.

Hitler may have known that the

DER FUEHRER'S FACE—Adolf Hitler, top photo, as he looked before he disappeared and three suggestions by Central Press Artist E. George Green of how No. 1 Nazi may have changed himself—if he is still alive and in hiding from wrath of an outraged world.

body of Attila the Hun disappeared after his death in 453. He became part of the Teutonic legend of Nibelungenlied, in which Siegfried also figures.

Although rumors have originated in Spain, Argentina, Italy, Japan and Sweden that mysterious movements of parties which might include Hitler have been seen, the hunt for him inside Germany itself has not relaxed.

The arrest of Gerlach Hemmerich, an ex-member of the German general staff and slated to be a defendant at Nuernberg, after he had worked incognito for four months in a United States Army billet in Berlin, highlighted the possibility of Nazi leaders going underground

report circulated for years that ... was not Lincoln's assassin. John Wilkes Booth, who was shot to death by Union soldiers in a barn 12 days after the assassination, but a sleeping tramp who was mistaken for Booth.

Up until a few years ago it was necessary for official denial to be made that Booth did not evade justice and live out his natural life.

One of the greatest international legends was that of the fabulous Marshal Ney, Napoleon's chief lieutenant and called by him "the bravest of the brave."

Did Ney Escape?

Although Ney was convicted by a French court-martial and officially executed on Dec. 8, 1815, in Luxembourg Gardens, the report circulated that the firing squad, former soldiers under Ney, purposely missed their aim and he was permitted to escape.

To this day there are historians who contend that Ney eventually escaped to the United States where many persons later reported seeing him in various disguises.

It is a string of these legends that Allied authorities want to forestall by uncovering conclusive proof that Hitler was slain or killed himself in the maelstrom of falling Berlin.

Meanwhile, there are those who remain convinced that Hitler lives. A leading public opinion poll reported only a few weeks ago that two out of three Americans still refuse to believe that Hitler is dead.

As the Nuernberg trial gets underway the absence of knowledge as to the precise fate or whereabouts of Hitler probably will become more of an aching void unless in the meantime some of the most sensational disclosures in a period of sensational world-shaking events are forthcoming.

Office Memorandum · UNITED STATES GOVERNMENT

TO : Mr. D. M. Ladd
FROM : Mr. E. C. Fitch
SUBJECT:
DATE: March 6, 1946

49583

There is attached hereto a brochure or book entitled "Adolf Hitler, Certificate of Marriage, Private Will and Political Testament." This brochure is prepared with the original document appearing on the left-hand side of the page and the English translation appearing on the right-hand side.

It is noted that the signatures of Adolf Hitler, Eva Hitler nee Braun, Joseph Goebbels and Martin Bormann are signed to the marriage certificate which signatures appear on page 2 of the marriage certificate. It is noted that the signatures of Adolf Hitler and signatures of Martin Bormann, Nicholaus Von Below, and Dr. Goebbels appear on page 3 of Hitler's private will. The name of Bormann appears on a letter prepared by Martin Bormann to the Grand Admiral. The signatures of Hitler, Dr. Joseph Goebbels, Wilhelm Burgdorf, Martin Bormann and Hans Krebs appear at the bottom of page 10 of Hitler's political testament.

The attached brochure was handed to ▓▓▓▓▓ of the Liaison Section by Colonel ▓▓▓▓, MIS. Colonel ▓▓▓▓ advised that the attached brochure was prepared by the Military Intelligence Service from captured documents, and was prepared in the attached form so that the Chief of Staff might give it to the President, who undoubtedly will eventually place it in the Library of Congress. Colonel ▓▓▓▓ advised ▓▓▓▓ that he had been advised by General Vandenberg that the Chief of Staff was delighted with the attached material, but was reluctant to pass it to the President until some attempts have been made to verify the authenticity of the documents and signature of Hitler.

There are also attached numerous documents which were captured by the Military Intelligence Service at the Headquarters of the Wehrmacht which contain copies of Hitler's signature in September, 1940; January, 1942; September, 1944; October 12, 1944; October 24, 1944 and December 15, 1944. There are also attached documents captured at the Headquarters of the Wehrmacht containing the signatures of M. Bormann and Burgdorf. There is also attached a folder dated September 22, 1939, containing Hitler's signature on page 2.

Colonel ▓▓▓▓ advised Mr. ▓▓▓▓ that General Vandenberg desired the Bureau to make a comparison of the signatures appearing in the attached book with those appearing on the attached official documents in order to ascertain whether or not the signature appearing on the alleged marriage certificate and wills are authentic. Colonel ▓▓▓▓ indicated to ▓▓▓▓ that the Chief of Staff desired that this information be obtained as expeditiously as possible. ▓▓▓▓ advised Colonel ▓▓▓▓ the matter would be handled special in the Bureau.

Colonel ▓▓▓▓ also cautioned ▓▓▓▓ that the information appearing in the book, that is, the fact that the Army has what appears to be Hitler's marriage certificate, private will and public testament, is not known at the present time, and it is desired that this matter be maintained secret by the Bureau.

57 APR 18 1946

REPORT of the FBI LABORATORY

FEDERAL BUREAU OF INVESTIGATION
WASHINGTON D. C.

65-53615-61   March 13, 1946

To: Assistant Chief of Staff, G-2
      War Department
      Washington, D. C.

                              Attention: ███████████

There follows the report of the FBI Laboratory on the examination of evidence received in the Bureau from Colonel ████████████ and submitted to the Laboratory on March 7, 1946.

                                                John Edgar Hoover, Director

Re: Adolf Hitler, Certificate of Marriage,
      Private Will and Political Testament;
      Examination for War Department.

                                          YOUR FILE NO.
                                          FBI FILE NO.
                                          LAB NO.   D-49553 AD

Examination requested by: Bureau

Reference: March 6, 1946

Examination requested: Document

The bound original papers:

"Adolf Hitler:
  Q1 - Q2   Certificate of Marriage
  Q3 - Q5   Private Will
  Q6 - Q17 Political Testament"

K1 - K14 Unquestioned captured documents containing signatures of Adolf Hitler, M. Bormann and Wilhelm Burgdorf.

Result of Examination:

For record purposes, each page of the questioned and each complete document of the known has been numbered as above.

                                                Continued next page

submitted which would exhibit all degrees of pressure and paper similar to Q3 to Q17 inclusive were used; K13 is a linen finish paper which is not smooth like Q3 through Q17.

4. Handwriting

From a comparison of the unquestioned and questioned signatures, it was concluded that the names A. Hitler, Bormann and Burgdorf on Q1 to Q17 inclusive are the genuine writings of the signers of the same names on K1 to K14 inclusive.

The remainder of the questioned signatures could not be completely analyzed as there are no known (except a printed reproduction of Goebbels) for comparison. These are: Eva Hitler (Braun), Hans Krebs, Nicolaus von Below, Joseph Goebbels. However, there is evidence that these are genuine signatures rather than drawings and no attempt to exhaust every possible means of analysis is considered necessary.

The Certificate of Marriage, Q1 and Q2, is prepared by filling in spaces on a typed form with written ink answers. However, the typing was not mechanically reproduced (as by Multigraph, Mimeograph or office Lithograph machines) and ordinary marriage forms even in war-torn Berlin are printed.

If a special form was typed for this particular ceremony, the natural thing to do would be to copy from the printed forms, modifying as needed but adhering to the legal provisos as much as possible, and using the typewriter for the blank spaces. The fact that the other documents are typed raises the question why this document is different.

Accordingly, the handwriting of the marriage paper was compared with the signatures. It was concluded that the "registrar" Walter Wagner, whose signature appears at the lower left of the paper, Q2, wrote the majority of the ink entries. The fact that certain entries were written in different ink and by other persons is evidence of the impromptu nature of the act. These entries (such as the identification of Eva Braun and the birth date of Bormann) were also compared with all of the signatures without effecting an identification. It is therefore concluded that the unusual way of preparing the document is evidence of genuineness rather than otherwise.

The original specimens, Q1 to Q17 inclusive and K1 to K14 inclusive, have been returned in person.

Office Memorandum · UNITED STATES GOVERNMENT
65-53615

TO : Mr. Harbo
FROM : J. A. Sizoo
SUBJECT: Adolf Hitler
Marriage Certificate
Private Will
Political Testament

DATE: March 27, 1946

In the above-entitled matter, one complete set of photographs is being made a part of the Laboratory file for record purposes. A second set of these photographs is retained in Room 7330 for <u>instructive purposes</u> in connection with the training of new technical employees of the Document Section. The third group of photographs is <u>attached hereto</u> for special filing in the event it is desirable at a later date to mount them for exhibit purposes.

A tickler of this memorandum is being set up for four months from this date, and the question of preparing a mounted folder will be resubmitted at that time.

CAA/mek

59 JUN 19 1946

EX - 25

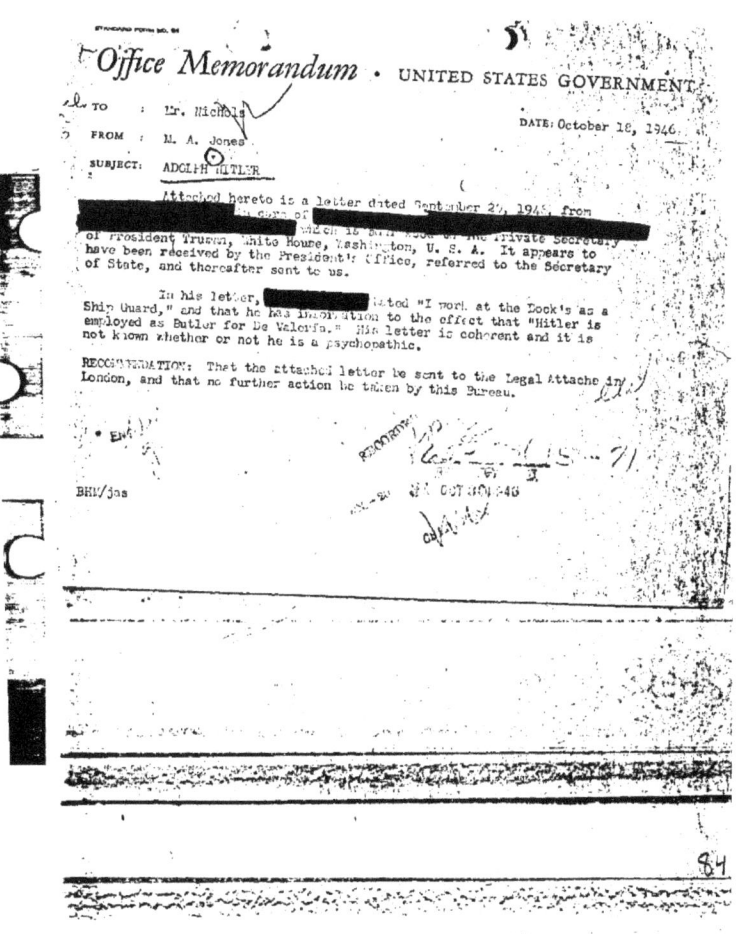

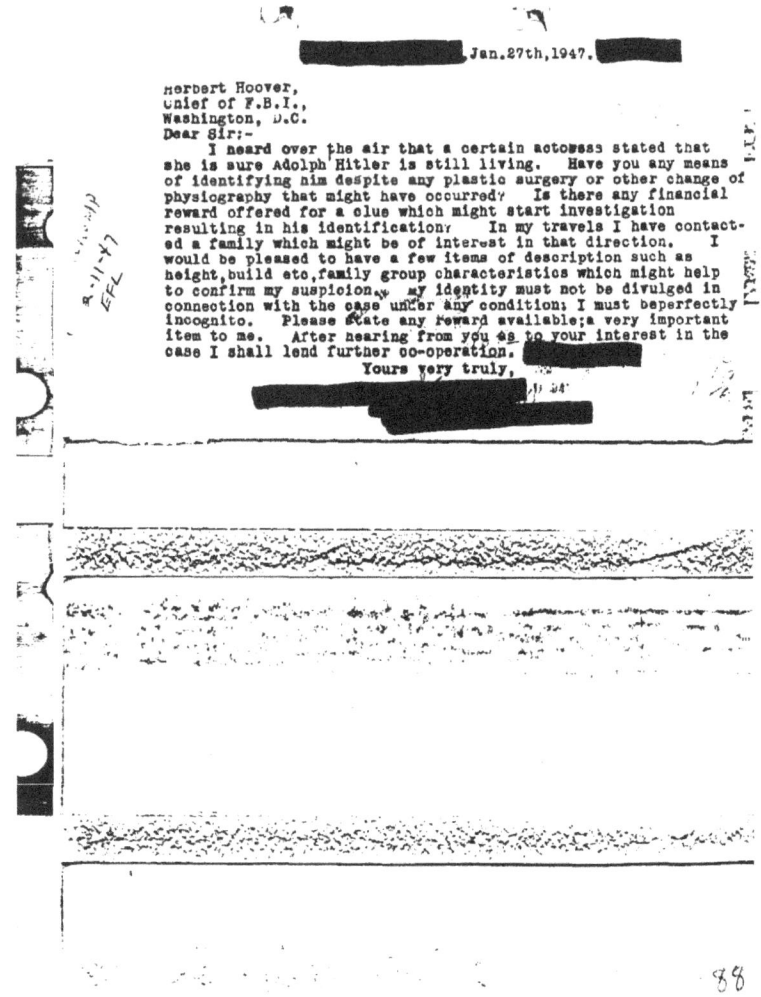

Jan. 27th, 1947.

Herbert Hoover,
Chief of F.B.I.,
Washington, D.C.
Dear Sir:-
    I heard over the air that a certain actoress stated that she is sure Adolph Hitler is still living. Have you any means of identifying him despite any plastic surgery or other change of physiography that might have occurred? Is there any financial reward offered for a clue which might start investigation resulting in his identification. In my travels I have contacted a family which might be of interest in that direction. I would be pleased to have a few items of description such as height, build etc, family group characteristics which might help to confirm my suspicion. My identity must not be divulged in connection with the case under any condition; I must be perfectly incognito. Please state any reward available; a very important item to me. After hearing from you as to your interest in the case I shall lend further co-operation.
                Yours very truly,

Office Memorandum • UNITED STATES GOVERNMENT

TO : DIRECTOR, FBI DATE: June 5, 1947
FROM : SAC, Los Angeles
SUBJECT: ADOLPH HITLER AND EVA BRAUN
INFORMATION CONCERNING

On May 16, 1947, ███ personally contacted the Los Angeles Office and advised that ███ desired to furnish the following information to Special Agent ███ with whom ███ personally acquainted. As Agent was not available, the following information was related to complaint Agent ███ story in substance is as follows:

On the evening of May 15, 1947 ███ was having dinner with a ███ the story which had been told to ███ by a ███ of the French underground of France during the German occupation of that country. ███ recently returned to the United States by way of Argentina and other South American countries, and when in one of these countries near Buenos Aires or Rio de Janeiro ███ was asked to give a ███ before some notables. ███ consented and was driven to a small community outside of Buenos Aires or Rio de Janeiro which was entirely populated by German people. ███ before a small gathering and at this gathering recognized EVA BRAUN and HITLER sitting at a table. ███ allegedly mentioned this recognition to ███ escort and was cautioned that ███ should not mention it on the outside or ███ life would be in danger.

███ subsequently identified to Agent WARREN the ███ as ███

███ was interviewed personally and ███ related substantially the same information furnished by ███ and disclosed the name of ███ as the ███ in question. The community where ███ allegedly saw HITLER and BRAUN was the town of Casino near Rio Grande, Brazil. ███ stated that the story had been related to ███ by ███ and sounded fantastic. ███ who ███ flew in and out of Berlin during the war, was of the opinion that there was no legal evidence of the death of HITLER and EVA BRAUN and that the story was entirely possible. Any reference hereinafter made to either ███ will refer to one and the same person.

___CTO__, FBI   June 5, 1947

Re: ADOLPH HITLER AND EVA BRAUN
    INFORMATION CONCERNING

▓▓▓▓▓▓▓▓▓▓ had been introduced to ▓▓▓▓▓▓ by ▓▓▓▓▓▓▓▓▓ ▓▓▓ at present is attempting to break into the industry as a ▓▓▓▓▓▓▓▓ who is of ▓▓▓▓ extraction also, described ▓▓▓ as a member of ▓▓▓ ▓▓▓▓▓▓▓▓▓ and described as being from a ▓▓▓▓▓▓▓▓▓▓▓▓ ▓▓▓▓ who was very active in the French Underground according to ▓▓▓▓▓ also said that ▓▓ who had recently arrived in town, was not accepted at first by the ▓▓▓ Colony until they found out who ▓▓ was and then the ▓▓▓ Consulate and numerous ▓▓ of prominence in the country began to "bow and scrape" to ▓▓.

Through a telephone contact with ▓▓▓▓▓▓▓ it was learned that the story had been given to ▓▓ in confidence and furthermore that the story had been furnished to the government officials by letter. ▓▓ stated that they had no objections of agents interviewing ▓▓ provided the latter was not advised as to the source of information.

On May 27, 1947 ▓▓▓▓ was interviewed by Special Agent ▓▓▓▓▓▓ LOS ANGELES. This room has been shared with ▓▓▓▓ during the latter's visit to this country. During the interview the following information was obtained:

▓▓▓▓▓▓▓▓▓▓▓▓▓▓▓▓▓▓▓▓▓▓▓▓▓▓▓▓▓▓▓▓ produced a passport, ▓▓▓▓▓▓▓▓ which contained visa ▓▓▓▓▓▓▓▓▓▓▓▓▓ Los Angeles, California, stamped May 1, 1947. The passport reflected numerous entries from various countries in South America and Europe, and the fact that ▓ was en route from Rio de Janeiro to Martinique, French possession, via Los Angeles.

▓▓▓▓▓▓▓▓▓▓ who spoke very broken English, was aided during this interview by ▓▓▓▓▓▓▓ who spoke partly fluent English. ▓▓ said that he was in the ▓▓▓▓▓▓▓▓▓▓ stating his ▓▓▓ owned a ▓▓▓▓▓▓▓▓▓ and that ▓ legal address was ▓▓▓▓▓▓▓▓▓▓▓▓▓ business address was ▓▓▓▓▓▓▓▓▓ was leaving Los Angeles on this date, May 27, 1947, at 5:00 p.m., by air for Martinique, where ▓ expected to be for a couple of months ▓▓ address was given as ▓▓▓▓▓▓ Martinique.

DIRECTOR, FBI   June 5, 1947

Re: ADOLPH HITLER AND EVA BRAUN
INFORMATION CONCERNING

▓▓▓▓▓▓▓▓▓▓▓▓▓▓▓▓▓▓▓▓▓▓▓▓▓▓▓▓▓▓▓▓▓▓

▓▓▓▓▓▓ passport further reflected that ▓▓▓▓▓▓ which ▓▓ explained as being a ▓▓▓▓▓▓ volunteered the information that ▓▓ was an amateur journalist and had aspirations toward being a writer. ▓▓ Main source of income, however, was from the ▓▓▓▓ mentioned above, ▓▓▓▓ claimed to be traveling throughout the world in this connection lining up merchandise for importing. ▓▓ claimed to have arrived in this country by air from Rio de Janeiro on March 9, 1947 at N.Y.C. and transacted business there until arriving in Los Angeles about the first of May.

At the outset of the interview ▓▓▓▓ mentioned that ▓▓ had been a ▓▓▓▓▓▓ and it was subsequently learned when ▓▓ produced certain papers for inspection that one of his letterheads carried the following information:

"GENERAL SECRETARY TO THE COMPANY: ▓▓▓▓▓▓▓▓▓

- 3 -

DIRECTOR, FBI   June 5, 1947

Re: ADOLPH HITLER AND EVA BRAUN
    INFORMATION CONCERNING

▓▓▓▓▓▓▓▓▓▓▓▓▓ about March 5, 1947, at least between the 1st and 5th
of March of this year, was in Brazil on business. ▓▓▓ had contacted
several newspapers in Brazil seeking information of interest to a journalist, and it became known that ▓▓▓ was also known as ▓▓▓▓▓▓▓▓▓▓
▓▓▓▓▓▓▓▓▓▓▓ Consequently ▓▓▓▓ by ▓▓▓▓▓▓▓
at Porto Alegra, Brazil, became interested in ▓▓▓▓▓▓▓
a group of notables in the Casino area.

Through this individual, ▓▓▓▓▓ was directed to a journalist
in Rio Grande, which is about fifteen miles from Casino and near the
Uruguayian border, Southeast Coast of Brazil. This journalist operates a
newspaper ▓▓▓▓▓▓
Through arrangements made by the latter journalist, whose name
did not remember, ▓▓▓ was sent to Casino with five ▓▓▓▓▓ to
give a ▓▓▓▓▓▓▓ was in charge and was to direct the ▓▓▓
This ▓▓▓▓ was to be held at the Grande Hotel de Casino on three
successive nights.

The ▓▓▓▓▓▓▓▓ included one American ▓▓▓ by the name of
▓▓▓▓▓ who ▓ said was well known at the Colonne Theatre, Buenos
Aires, South America; a Russian ▓▓▓▓▓ who was a famous
▓▓▓▓▓▓▓▓ and the names of the other three
▓▓▓▓ did not remember, but one was an Australian, another
Nicaraguan, and the other French. ▓▓ had no negotiations with the
booking of these ▓▓▓ consequently was not advised too much as to
their background with the exception of the two named above.

Upon arrival at Casino, described as a community of approximately
five thousand people, it occurred to ▓▓▓▓ that this was an unusual
community inasmuch as it was necessary for the ▓▓▓ to secure a pass to
enter the vicinity of the town, and furthermore it was practically of
one hundred percent German population. This area also lacked commercial
establishments and consisted of villas or homes and a large hotel which had
been remodeled and was very modern. It appeared in size out of proportion
to the size of the community.

- 4 -

..., FBI   June 5, 1947

Re: ADOLPH HITLER AND EVA BRAUN
    INFORMATION CONCERNING
    ▓▓▓▓▓▓▓▓▓▓▓▓▓▓▓▓▓▓▓▓▓▓▓▓▓

    At the hotel no identification was necessary nor was it necessary for the ▓▓▓▓▓ register. They were shown directly to their rooms. The manager was very courteous to the ▓▓▓▓ as well as were the townspeople, with the exception of the Russian ▓▓▓ who was apparently well known. ▓▓ received no cordial reception and felt a little out of place in view of ▓▓ nationality. The rest of the ▓▓ including ▓▓ were invited into the various homes of the inhabitants and were engaged in social conversation frequently.

    One thing of unusual interest came to the attention of ▓▓▓ at Casino when one of the ▓▓▓▓ reported a large radio station near the hotel. This station was peculiar in that the antenna which was quite lengthy was parallel to the ground instead of perpendicular. It was fenced off but could be observed from the street and the buildings nearby, having some sort of electrical equipment inasmuch as ▓▓▓ heard a dynamo but did not actually see the equipment. ▓▓ described the location of this radio station as follows: "When standing in front of the hotel take the first boulevard to the right and a short distance away the first path or narrow street which cuts to the left. Turn left and walk approximately from five to seven minutes and the equipment may be observed."

    The ▓▓▓ was advertised in Casino and was to be given at three performances in successive evenings. The performances were to be held in a hotel, combination ballroom and theatre, which would seat several hundred people.

    ▓▓▓ observed one of the maids in the hotel speaking to a young girl approximately seventeen years of age who was attractive and had chestnut colored hair. This young girl gave a "heil HITLER salute" to one of the hotel servants, which ▓▓▓ thought was of particular interest. It was further learned that the hotel owner also had interest in a cafe and club known as "The Jockey Club" at Casino and also had interest in a large manufacturing plant about half way between Casino and Rio Grande. This plant manufactured woolen and other types of goods. The inhabitants of Casino did not appear to be engaged in any particular occupation.

- 5 -

DIRECTOR, FBI   June 5, 1947

Re: ADOLPH HITLER AND EVA BRAUN
    INFORMATION CONCERNING

    Near the middle of the table ▓ observed a woman whom ▓ immediately felt ▓ had seen before. In refreshing ▓ memory ▓ suddenly arrived at the conclusion that she was EVA BRAUN of whom ▓ had observed many photographs but had never seen in person. Upon recognizing this woman ▓ felt that HITLER might be nearby and examined more closely the other members of the group sitting at the large table. There was one man in particular having numerous characteristics of HITLER. This man was described as having the same general build and age of HITLER, was clean-shaven, and had a very short German crew haircut. This man was rather emaciated and ▓ ▓ felt that this party was definitely HITLER, but ▓ was not as sure as ▓ was that the woman described above was EVA BRAUN. The HITLER suspect appeared to be friendly with everyone at the table.

    After the performance, which was well received, dancing was held and a number of people including guests at the hotel and those at the large table remained for dancing. It was noticed that the young girl stayed with an elderly woman most of the time. However, ▓ was introduced to the young girl and ▓ ▓. She was very talkative in German, gay, and rather proud. She seemed to want to impress ▓. This girl had, during one of the intermissions, given ▓ a bank note as a sort of gratuity for a fine performance and stated that she hoped ▓ would keep it for a souvenir.

    ▓ learned the name of the young girl was ABAVA (phonetic) and she claimed to be a German but was now a Chilian and resided in Chile. ▓ mentioned that these people who claimed to be Chilian spoke German entirely and there was no evidence of the Spanish or Portuguese language being used, which made ▓ doubt that they had not resided in that section of the country very long.

    During the next day ▓ and ▓ further circulated in the village and ▓ took a trip out to the aforementioned manufacturing plant near Rio Grande, ▓ further noticed that everyone spoke German.

    During the performance of the second evening at the hotel, the same table was set up but on this evening the table contained an extra chair and as of the previous evening the occupants of the table came in late. ▓ again observed the girl whom ▓ thought to be EVA BRAUN and the young girl but did not observe the man whom ▓ judged to be HITLER on the previous evening. ▓ did notice a very large man of approximately fifty

- 7 -

Federal Bureau of Investigation
United States Department of Justice
Washington, D. C.

American Embassy
1, Grosvenor Square
London, W. 1
October 31, 1947

VIA AIR POUCH

Director, FBI
Washington, D. C.

Dear Sir:

Re: THE RUMORED POISONING OF HITLER .

    There is attached for the information of the Bureau, copy of OI Special Report No. 53 (OI-SR/53) dated October 4, 1947. This report contains a series of arguments to prove that Dr. Morell, physician to Hitler, did not give poison to him or administer narcotics in any quantity which might have contributed to the impairment of Hitler's health.

    The statements to disprove the rumors about Morell were made by people who knew Hitler and by scientists or chemists who examined the drugs which Morell administered to Hitler. The rumor that Morell was poisoning Hitler was started by Giesing, a physician who had access to Hitler for a while after July 20, 1944, and who, together with Dr. Brandt, probably wished to get rid of the obnoxious Morell.

    It is also argued that Hitler inherited certain traits which manifested themselves in childhood and later on, and that these might account for his crimes and other actions.

    This report was made abailable to me by AC of S, G-2, Frankfurt, Germany, and copies of same are not being retained in the files of this office.

                            Very truly yours,

                            J. A. Cimperman
                            Legal Attaché

JAC:LH
65-600
Enclosure

INSPECTOR, FBI   June 5, 1947

Re: ADOLPH HITLER AND EVA BRAUN
    INFORMATION CONCERNING

came to New York and subsequently to Los Angeles where
visited with ▓▓▓▓ Colony and was staying with
▓▓▓▓ felt that ▓▓▓ should furnish to the authorities in some
manner the results of ▓▓ experience in Casino. ▓▓ was afraid to furnish
it to the ▓▓▓ as he said he did not trust them. ▓▓ felt
that ▓▓ would also like to somewhat protect ▓▓ identity as a source of
information to this government. ▓▓ took into confidence several of
friends in Hollywood, among them ▓▓ the others ▓▓ did not identify.
One of these friends recommended that ▓▓ write a letter to DREW PEARSON,
the writer of a Washington, D. C. newspaper column, "Washington Merry Go
Round". It was explained that PEARSON had governmental connections and
would see that the information reached the proper authorities. Subsequently,
with the aid of ▓▓▓▓▓▓ a letter in ▓▓▓ was drafted and forwarded
to DREW PEARSON on May 13, 1947 setting forth in substance the story related
to agents.

▓▓▓▓▓▓▓▓▓▓▓ believed that agents contacted them with
regards to this letter and in view of this fact agents were able to fully
protect their source of information, namely, ▓▓▓▓▓

Both ▓▓▓ were very cordial and fully cooperative
during the interview, which was rather rushed, as ▓▓ was getting ready
to leave for Martinique. ▓▓ was observed leaving ▓▓ residence
accompanied by ▓▓ another individual who was a young ▓▓ approximately twenty-one years of age, who was driving a 1941 Chevrolet convertible
coupe bearing California license for 1947, ▓▓▓▓. This car is registered
to ▓▓▓▓ North Hollywood, the legal owner.
The following is the description of ▓▓▓

    Age
    Height
    Weight
    Sex
    Race
    Hair
    Eyes
    Complexion
    Features

- 10 -

___CTOR, FBI   June 5, 1947

Re: ADOLPH HITLER AND EVA BRAUN
    INFORMATION CONCERNING

    The Los Angeles Office indices reflect no record of the above mentioned individuals who made available the data contained in this communication.

    The possibilities that ▓▓▓▓ may be a Communist Party courier or Russian agent are being considered. This belief is taken in view of ▓▓▓▓ widespread travels, ▓▓▓▓ claimed French Underground connections, and ▓▓▓▓ organization wh.c▓▓ apparently maintains at ▓▓▓▓ as reflected on the letterhead herein described.

    Any subsequent information developed in this case or in relation ▓▓▓▓ activities will be appropriately furnished to the Bureau.

LFW:EKT
62-0

- 12 -

Real Estate, Loans and Insurance

Elizabethton, Tennessee
June 2ᴅ 1947

Mr. J. Edgar Hoover, Chief of F.B.I.
Washington, D.C.

Dear Mr. Hoover:

In a paper or magazine recently I saw a poll on whether Hitler was alive and maybe in this country. In looking through our files this morning I came across some correspondence that by the merest chance might be of help if Hitler should be hiding here.

████████ was in Wytheville, Virginia and we heard he was in Black Mountain, North Carolina. We did not hear from him any more, telegrams, phone calls, letters were not answered after he went to North Carolina. We assumed he bought a farm there, possibly the one we wrote him about.

Jesse Jones, big man in Roosevelt's administration, his brother owned the farm we wrote ████ about. Mr. Jones brother is a doctor and I think lives in Waco, Texas.

In reading my letter looks like I got the cart before the horse, correspondence I am enclosing will explain.

I am one of many others that thinks Hitler is still alive, and possibly here in the good country we are so fortunate as to live in.

truly yours,

```
C
O
P
Y
```

La Martinique 13 June 1947

To
Special agents ▮▮▮▮▮ & ▮▮▮▮▮
Federal Bureau of Investigation
510 South Spring Street
LOS ANGELES - California - USA -

Dear Sirs,

   I have the pleasure to insert in that letter, the summary of our meeting in Los Angeles the 27th of May 1947.
   We leave in a few days for BOGOTA in Colombia. If you want an inquiry, you can send a cable or a letter to the American Consul of Bogota, we'll go to ask him if he received a message for us.
   We'll stay about two in BOGOTA, and leave after the 15th of July.
   ▮▮▮▮▮ does not come very soon in the States, but I believe after my trip, come for a few days in Los Angeles. You can leave a message at the same address: ▮▮▮▮▮ and you tell to the Lady of the house, she doesn't forward, she has to keep that letter and give me when I come back.
   I remain dear Sirs

                              Yours faithfully

                              /s/ ▮▮▮▮▮

                  Ex Officer in the Free French forces

SAC, Los Angeles   August 29, 1947

Director, FBI

ADOLPH HITLER AND EVA BRAUN
INFORMATION CONCERNING
                    ALSO KNOWN AS
                    INFORMANT

Reference is made to your letter to the Bureau dated June 5, 1947, in the above captioned matter.

There is enclosed copy of a letter to the Bureau from Rio de Janeiro, Brasil, dated August 6, 1947, reflecting investigation of this matter. Photostatic copies of letters which were furnished to the Bureau as enclosures with this letter advise that ▓▓▓▓▓ and ▓▓▓▓▓ were travelling in Martinique, French West Indies, at which time they contacted the American Consular Service and furnished to them a report addressed to Special Agents ▓▓▓▓▓ and ▓▓▓▓▓, Federal Bureau of Investigation, 510 South Spring Street, Los Angeles, California, U.S.A. It was requested that the report be forwarded through special channels to avoid possible censorship. This report, which is in French is apparently a summary of the information furnished by ▓▓▓▓▓ to your office. ▓▓▓▓▓ and ▓▓▓▓▓ seemed to have plenty of money and signified their intentions of visiting several South American countries.

The American Consulate in Martinique conducted an investigation of these two men inasmuch as they were supposed to be representing a motion picture firm in Hollywood, California which was interested in making a motion picture based on a story of Martinique. It was supposed to have a cast of 23 persons. The fact that they were interested in leaving the country before the cast arrived aroused suspicion. The investigation revealed that ▓▓▓▓▓ was wanted in Paris for passing bad checks in 1946 and since he was in London at that time, he was indicted, tried and sentenced in absentia. The Governor of Martinique intended to place the men under arrest and return them to Paris. The local court pointed out that these men could not be held by the Martinique authorities until the evidence in the case arrived from Paris. Knowing this, ▓▓▓▓▓ attempted to depart from the Island for the United States inasmuch as he had a valid visa for this country. He was unsuccessful in obtaining immediate passage. The American Consul suggested that he would cancel this visa if the passport were brought to him.

Rio de Janeiro, Brazil
August 6, 1947

SECRET - AIR COURIER

Director, FBI

Re: ADOLPH HITLER AND EVA BRAUN
INFORMATION CONCERNING

Dear Sir:

Reference is made to Bureau letter dated July 9, 1947 bearing the above-captioned title.

███████ in the State of Rio Grande Do Sul, advised that the town referred to as Casino is a suburb of the city of Rio Grande. This suburb commonly is referred to as Casino, although it is a part of the municipality of Rio Grande. ███████ advised that Casino was located in a summer resort area and that it consisted of approximately two hundred scattered residences. The majority of the inhabitants are German nationals or are of German descent.

According to ███████ it could be expected that a Nazi refugee would seek asylum or assistance in the Casino area because of the existence of the predominantly German element. The center of activity in Casino is a large hotel which includes a gambling casino. Since gambling has been prohibited, the hotel manager from time to time has endeavored to arrange some form of entertainment for guests and visitors from nearby Rio Grande. It may be pointed out that the Casino section is on the coast and that the beach which borders the suburb regularly is frequented by residents of the city of Rio Grande.

With regard to the alleged necessity for passes to travel in the area of Casino, it is believed that the allegation is without specific foundation. For the information of the Bureau, foreign nationals in Brazil are required by law to possess "carteiras de identidade", which are identification cards issued officially by the Brazilian Government. Often when traveling from one city to another by automobile police may request drivers and passengers to exhibit their identification cards or their passports. Such a request may be

ENCLOSURE ATTACHED

Re: ADOLPH HITLER and EVA BRAUN

predicated upon a routine police investigation. In the instant case, it is possible that the police may have received some derogatory report regarding ▓▓▓▓▓

For the information of the Bureau, ▓▓▓▓ advised that files of the Rio Police Department disclosed the following data regarding ▓▓▓▓ described in the referenced letter:

███████████████████████████████████████
███████████████████████████████████████
███████████████████████████████████████
███████████████████████████████████████

Mr. ARTHUR FOLEY, American Vice Consul at Rio, advised that the Embassy had received information from FREDERICK D. HUNT, American Consul, Martinique, F.W.I., reflecting that ▓▓▓▓ and ▓▓▓▓ had arrived in Martinique and their presence in that city led to a series of communications, photostatic copies of which are enclosed herewith and described as follows:

1. Letter dated June 13, 1947 from FREDERICK D. HUNT, American Consul, Martinique, F.W.I. to Ambassador PAWLEY, Rio de Janeiro, enclosing (1) copy of letter dated June 13, 1947 at Martinique to Special Agents ▓▓▓▓ and ▓▓▓▓ from ▓▓▓▓; and (2) copy of a report written in the French language signed by ▓▓▓▓.

2. Letter dated June 17, 1947 from FREDERICK D. HUNT, American Consul, Martinique, to Ambassador PAWLEY, Rio de Janeiro.

3. Copy of a letter dated June 25, 1947 at Martinique from FREDERICK D. HUNT to the State Department.

4. Letter dated June 30, 1947 at Martinique from FREDERICK D. HUNT to Ambassador PAWLEY.

-2-

DIRECTOR, FBI   9/23/47

It bore the return address of ▓▓▓▓▓▓▓ San Francisco Calif." The communication transmitted therein is quoted as follows:

"Dear Sir   It seems to me that the radio public are well 'fed up' with soap - opera - halitosis and B.C. and would welcome a change. When I took my 5th and last trip to Europe in 1932 I met A. Hitler through ▓▓▓▓▓ for the ▓▓▓▓▓ FRANKFURTER ZEITUNG, one of Europe's most famous journals. Last summer I received (enclosed) letter from H. call it Hitler hoax if you will and believe its delivery in German over a USA radio would be the most startling sensation since Orson Welles 'attack of the martians'----

"If interested, let me know and I can come over about further details.

"Sincerely

The enclosure mentioned therein was an envelope addressed ▓▓▓▓▓ It bore the return address of "After Nov. 1945 return to Adolf Hitler, Reichskanzler - Berlin".

Inside the envelope was an English translation of the purported letter in German which ▓▓▓▓ had allegedly received from HITLER in said envelope. The translation is set forth as follows:

"Translation of Hitler's Letter

"(Also Enclosed)

- 2 -

DIRECTOR, FBI   9/23/47

"No doubt it is well known that little has happened in my life that could be called laughable, but when at the time of the Russian attack on Berlin I found refuge in the basement of the Imperial Chancellory building I was informed that my body and that of my wife (nee Eva Braun) had been covered with naptha and burned in the Chancellory garden. I could not help smiling for at this time we were many kilometers south west of Berlin on our air journey to Argentina and my friend PERON, on a "Condor" Line plane loaned me with a crew of two by a South American Republic.

"I have no sympathy with the Christlegend nor the anti Semitics who call all of Jewry Christ Killers, but I do know that every country is cursed with the number and kind of Jews it deserves and will suffer from them until it expells them - or else ----

"I wish only to add that my friend BORNEMANN was many years active in Sweden preparing all for the recovery of our party and a closer approach to our ideals. Even if heads must roll again.

"In the mean time I am

/s/ Adolf Hitler
Reichskangler
Berlin --- "

Examination of the envelope addressed to ▓▓▓ bearing HITLER's purported return address in Berlin disclosed it bore two cancelled German postage stamps but no postmark on the envelope itself. It was also observed the handwriting appearing thereon is quite similar to ▓▓▓ handwriting as contained in the other letters described above. ▓▓▓ was accordingly interviewed by Special Agents ▓▓▓ at ▓▓▓ office, ▓▓▓ San Francisco, California. ▓▓▓ readily admitted having personally addressed to ▓▓▓ the envelope bearing the German stamps, that ▓▓▓ had taken two cancelled German postage stamps from another envelope and glued them thereon and that ▓▓▓ reason for attempting to perpetrate this hoax was to create a sensation. ▓▓▓ is 77 years old and seemed to be a psychopathic case. ▓▓▓ face flushed and ▓▓▓ eyes became glassy and ▓▓▓ stated had a weak heart. The interview was discontinued upon ▓▓▓ assurance that ▓▓▓ had made no other similar efforts in the past and that ▓▓▓ would attempt no further hoaxes in the future.

- 3 -

Office Memorandum · UNITED STATES GOVERNMENT

TO : Director, FBI
DATE: February 10, 1948
FROM : SAC, Atlanta
SUBJECT: WHEREABOUTS OF ADOLPH HITLER
MISCELLANEOUS

Recently while ▓▓▓▓▓ was conducting an investigation concerning another matter at Rome, Georgia, ▓▓▓▓▓ Rome, Georgia, furnished the following information. ▓▓▓ stated that ▓▓▓ served with the Army in Germany after the close of hostilities and around Christmas of 1945 ▓▓▓ was in a village of Schwindigg which is located near Muhldorf. While in company with a German by the name of ▓▓▓ last name unknown, ▓▓▓ visited a tourist home at Schwindigg whose owner was a member of the Nazi Party and exhibited his membership certificate. This individual stated that the information concerning HITLER being dead is entirely erroneous and that HITLER was nearby Schwindigg. ▓▓▓ continued that later in the evening ▓▓▓ went to a tavern about one and a half to two miles from Schwindigg in the direction of a range of mountains. While at this tavern, ▓▓▓ engaged in conversation with several Germans and although they were drinking, at least two or three of them remarked ▓▓▓ that HITLER was not dead but was nearby.

▓▓▓ advised that the area near Schwindigg is very mountainous and of a rough terrain and that ▓▓▓ opinion is that a person would be able to hide out in that area indefinitely with a certain amount of help from persons nearby.

This letter is being furnished for information purposes only.

62-0
TBP:aej

Office Memorandum · UNITED STATES GOVERNMENT

TO : Mr. D. M. LADD
FROM : James H. Merritt
SUBJECT : ADOLF HITLER and woman aboard City of New Orleans, Ill. Central Railroad, 2/28/48

DATE: February 28, 1948
Time of call: 11:35 P.M., 2/28/48

SAC POSTER telephonically advised the writer that ███████████, had called him and advised as follows: ███████ flagman on the Illinois Central Railroad, boarded the City of New Orleans, a train which left New Orleans at 8:00 A.M. today, at Cairo, Illinois, at 8:02 P.M., Central Standard Time, tonight. On this train ███████ observed a man in Seat 40, Car 10, whom he believed was ADOLF HITLER. This individual was accompanied by a woman. ███████ described the man as follows:

  Height   5'11"
  Weight   180 pounds
  Age   59 to 60
  Hair   Dark brown
  Wearing a brown double-breasted suit
  Small light mustache
  Extremely nervous
  Spoke in both English and German. Had heavy German accent.

███████ described the woman as follows:

  Age   41
  Weight   135 pounds
  Hair   Dark brown turning gray
  Green dress with "new look"

POSTER advised that ███████ Special Agent of the Illinois Central Railroad was also aboard this train and that he observed these individuals and substantiated ███████ story. POSTER stated that ███████ was sober and claimed that ███████ and ███████ were also.

POSTER stated that it was not possible due to the lack of time to have one of his Agents board this train, and that he had called ███████ at Champaign, Illinois, and ███████ at Kankakee, Illinois, who are both very friendly to the Bureau, and asked them to board the train and observe these individuals and report back to him. POSTER stated that he also called SAC McSWAIN in Chicago as the train was due to arrive at one station in Chicago at 11:43 P.M., CST, and at another station in Chicago at 11:55 P.M. POSTER stated that McSWAIN advised that he would have Agents cover both stations, and observe these individuals, and that McSWAIN would call the Bureau and report their findings.

VHM:kk

POSTER informed that he thought the Bureau might have some inquiries on this matter from the press as the information was known to the employees of the Illinois Central Railroad.

I called Mr. COYNE, Mr. FLETCHER, and Mr. McQUIRE and advised them of the above matter.

ADDENDUM: E.F. LANE on duty 12:45 A.M.
2/29/48

ASAC KELLY of the Springfield Office stated ▒▒▒▒ of Champaign, Illinois, advised that two men had left the train at Champaign for a short time but boarded the train again when it left.

▒▒▒▒▒▒▒▒ of Kankakee, Illinois, advised ASAC KELLY that six or seven persons had left the train at Kankakee but none fitted the descriptions of the individuals in question. ▒▒▒▒ also checked Car 10 of the train and found Seat 40 empty. ASAC KELLY stated this was not too significant as he was previously told that the man and woman involved had spent most of the day in the club car which was not checked by

- 2 -

Office Memorandum · UNITED STATES GOVERNMENT

TO : Mr. D. M. Ladd
FROM : H. B. Fletcher
SUBJECT: ADOLF HITLER and woman aboard City of New Orleans, Ill. Central Railroad, 2/28/48
DATE: March 3, 1948

At 4:30 pm today, I called SAC McSwain in Chicago in accord with your instructions with reference to the memorandum of February 28, 1948, relating to the identification of a passenger on the above-described train as being Adolf Hitler.

Mr. McSwain stated that this was washed out; that two Special Agents, ▓▓ and ▓▓▓▓▓▓, had got on the train and had closely observed the person in question and his woman companion. It was so obvious to the Agents that this person was not Adolf Hitler that they did not make a positive determination of his identity, feeling that it would possibly create a situation causing absurd publicity. He stated that the person in question was not more than 42; that instead of a foreign accent, he had a very pronounced southern accent; he wore a brown mustache; and his general appearance and over-all description precluded any possibility of his being identical with Adolf Hitler. The woman accompanying him, who had previously been stated to be 41 years old, in the opinion of Agents ▓▓ and ▓▓▓▓ could not have been more than 22 or 23. She was much younger than her reported description and she had no foreign accent whatever.

HBF:ecb

Federal Bureau of Investigation
United States Department of Justice
Washington, D. C.

American Embassy
1, Grosvenor Square
London, W. 1
October 31, 1947

VIA AIR POUCH

Director, FBI
Washington, D. C.

Dear Sir:

Re: THE RUMORED POISONING OF HITLER

There is attached for the information of the Bureau, copy of OI Special Report No. 53 (OI-SR/53) dated October 4, 1947. This report contains a series of arguments to prove that Dr. Morell, physician to Hitler, did not give poison to him or administer narcotics in any quantity which might have contributed to the impairment of Hitler's health.

The statements to disprove the rumors about Morell were made by people who knew Hitler and by scientists or chemists who examined the drugs which Morell administered to Hitler. The rumor that Morell was poisoning Hitler was started by Giesing, a physician who had access to Hitler for a while after July 20, 1944, and who, together with Dr. Brandt, probably wished to get rid of the obnoxious Morell.

It is also argued that Hitler inherited certain traits which manifested themselves in childhood and later on, and that these might account for his crimes and other actions.

This report was made available to me by AC of S, G-2, Frankfurt, Germany, and copies of same are not being retained in the files of this office.

Very truly yours,

J. A. Cimperman
Legal Attaché

JAC:LH
65-600
Enclosure

Office Memorandum • UNITED STATES GOVERNMENT

TO : Director, FBI DATE: May 6, 1948
FROM : SAC, Detroit
SUBJECT: INTERNAL SECURITY - G
Concerning Person possibly identical with ADOLPH HITLER

On April 26, 1948, a Special Agent attached to the Detroit Office interviewed ▓▓▓▓▓▓▓▓▓▓▓▓▓▓▓▓▓▓▓▓▓▓▓▓▓▓▓, Detroit, Michigan, at the request of ▓▓▓▓▓▓▓▓▓ who had previously communicated with the Detroit Office by telephone. ▓▓▓▓▓▓▓▓▓▓▓ produce broker, ▓▓▓▓▓▓▓ he conducts from his home address in Detroit, stated that from August 8 to August 17, 1946, he and his wife resided at Hotel Chicoutimi, Chicoutimi, Province of Quebec, which he described as being a very isolated and remote section of the province. On the first day of their arrival they were dumbfounded by the appearance of a man in the hotel lobby who appeared identical in every respect with ADOLPH HITLER.

This unknown person was described as 5'10-1/2" to 11" and weighing 185 to 190 pounds. There was no attempt at disguise. During their short period of residence they never saw this unknown person in company of other people except after 11 p.m. in the evening when four or five other visitors and the unknown individual would play chess in the lobby.

▓▓▓▓▓▓ further advised that the suspicions of his wife and himself were intensified by the following enumerated peculiar circumstances:

1. While no concrete evidence existed the ▓▓▓▓▓ felt that they were being spied upon and information as to their activities was being obtained by the unknown person.

2. Upon their arrival they encountered an American colonel and his family consisting of his wife and two children. They were struck by the apparent newness of the colonel's uniform which had the appearance of never having been worn before and by the distinct European dress of his wife and children.

3. The apparent effort of several other men in the community to groom their hair and mustaches to form the general appearance similar with ADOLPH HITLER. It was felt by the ▓▓▓▓ that this was an effort to divert suspicion from the individual whom they encountered at the hotel.

4. Upon returning to that section of Canada in 1947 the ▓▓▓▓▓ found no evidence of their original suspect nor did any of the local residents discuss him. In addition, those people whom they recall as grooming themselves similar to HITLER had in the meantime changed their looks.

Letter to Director, FBI Re: INTERNAL SECURITY - G
May 6, 1948   Concerning Person possibly identical
                  with ADOLFH HITLER

        ▆▆▆ indicated that he would be glad to cooperate with the Bureau in any way that it may so see fit. He also indicated a willingness to return to Canada if so desired by the Bureau.

        This letter is set forth for the purpose of information and there will be no further investigation by the Detroit Office.

WFD:WAC
100-

TRANSLATION FROM THE SPANISH

Investigation Department
Washington, D.C. – U.S.A.

Mexico, May 30, 1948

Hasn't Adolph Hitler died? This is the hope of every Investigator in the United States because none of them have been able to locate the hiding-place of the German Dictator.

They will never succeed in locating it because enormous difficulties stand in the way of the most expert detectives. It is useless for them to wander about the world trying to find a trace or clue which might lead them to the most discussed man in the world.

This does not refer to detectives who are trying to discover more detailed clues regarding the disappearance of the German Dictator.

The only person who can clarify the situation for them is a young man by the name of NRINGEHFTHJY EBBEXTROR (this must refer to Joachim von Ribbentrop). However, a huge fortune is involved – it would cost them about twenty million dollars to obtain the information.

For this sum of money, this young man will supply them with detailed information relating to the whereabouts of the man for whom the allies are conducting an intensive search. The young man who can supply this information is in the city of ANWQEEDSCAZX.

Adolph Hitler is neither in Spain nor in Argentina.

The point is that the youngest marshal in the German Army bears the name of NRINGEHFTHY EBBETROR (see above). Will he surrender Adolph Hitler and Eva Braun alive?

For a better world.

A servant,
/s/ HASDESXZFC EBGFOIJIU M.

Translated by:
June 7, 1948.

COPY   COPY

Mr. Hoover:

You have a 50-50 chance finding _Hittler_ in this location. I _seen_ a man 2 years back get out of a box car, the very image of _Hittler_ _hee_ wanted to find a man he _faugt_ with World _Ware_ I under the _Kiser_. I should of let you know a long _tim_ ago. I am alone. _Have_ seen him and he _dodeged_ out of sight.

Hope you can send some _won_.

                          Yors Res

From the _depo_.
Coast 3 house
when you cross the _Hi way_ (will tell you more).

              C
               O
                P
                 Y

TRANSLATION FROM THE SPANISH

Photostatic copy of article which appeared in "Nueva York Al Dia" (New York Day by Day), Spanish newspaper published in New York City.

Saturday, May 22, 1948.

Headline on first page: IT IS RUMORED THAT HITLER IS IN BOGOTA.
(article on page 5).

A fantastic letter provides details which are arousing curiosity in the most skeptical persons.

The newspaper " Nueva York Al Dia" reproduces the letter sent to the newspaper "El Tiempo" in Bogota, by the unidentified person who signed "Amigo, amigo, amigo". The letter is addressed from Oranjestad, Island of Aruba, and dated April 27, 1948.

The writer baldly states that HITLER IS NOW IN BOGOTA. "Amigo, amigo, amigo" claims that Hitler is in perfect health. He last saw Hitler about ten days ago. As soon as war breaks out between the United States and Russia, Hitler plans to set himself up as head of the western world. He hopes to gather together an army of five million men in the western hemisphere, in order to lead a general crusade against Bolshevism. "Amigo, amigo, amigo" asserts that Hitler has declared that " If war breaks out about two thirds of the population of the world may succumb, but there will be sufficient astronomical space left to allow the conquerors to extend toward sidereal paths where they will enjoy abiding greatness and peace."

"Amigo, amigo, amigo" claims that Hitler aspires to the conquest of the Moon and Mars, after he has completely defeated Russia.

"Amigo, amigo, amigo" provides the following data re the arrival of Hitler in Bogota, Colombia:-

Hitler landed from submarine "R.V.Z.- 1048" in Bahiahonda, coast of Guajira in Colombia, at dawn of July 19, 1945. He was accompanied by six men; two of them were radio and precision instrument experts; two were lieutenant colonels, one of them an infantry officer, and the other an artillery officer; one man was a major in the air corps, and the last was a submarine expert. All of them were garbed in civilian clothes, disguised as peasants. They carried equipment covered with oilskin, and canvas bags containing American dollars and \ls amounting to three million dollars. The money was hidden in household bn etc.

When the "group" landed at Bahiahonda they were met by four strong Guajiros Indians who were awaiting them at a special spot in order to guide them and their equipment to arranged places. Two agents or contact men came with these Indians. They had arranged everything in advance, and had horses and a truck waiting close by. Hitler and his escort had a very arduous trip. They were forced to travel at night and sometimes at early dawn. Finally, they arrived at a small port in Magdalena. Here they boarded small cargo boats or barges and travelled to another port in the same Department. They travelled third class. From the capital of Santander to Pamplona they travelled again by truck, and from Pamplona to Bogota they travelled by special car. They never stopped at any hotel of any type. The contact men or liaison agents took charge of getting passage on boats, etc. and of providing transportation and provisions. Trucks and other vehicles were always boarded at isolated places which were at quite a distance from any towns or cities.

"Amigo, amigo, amigo" states that Hitler is an avid movie fan, and has frequented movies from the time of his arrival in Bogota, Colombia.

He affirms that Hitler wore eyeglasses and a heavy beard at first, which gave him the appearance of an apathetic foreigner who seemed to be of delicate health.

(article is supposedly continued on page 18 of the newspaper. This page is not enclosed. - translator's note).

Summarized by:
Rose R. Offenbacher
July 28, 1948. RRO

TRANSLATION FROM THE SPANISH

Photostatic copy of article which appeared in "El Tiempo", Spanish newspaper published in Bogota, Columbia.

June 20, 1948.

Fantasy or Reality Concerning Hitler.-
SENSATIONAL ASSERTIONS RE THE FUEHRER IN BOGOTA.

A Colombian confirms the story told by "Amigo, amigo, amigo".

The voyage by submarine, the death of Eva Braun and the landing in Florida.- The death of Gaitán would have been a master coup against Communism on Hitler's part.- The plan "becomes hazy" - the musical key. Colombians took part in the adventure. Hitler has already disappeared from the savanna of Bogota.

In our edition of May we published a strange and sensational letter, postmarked Curaçao and signed by "Amigo, amigo, amigo" (Friend, friend, friend). In it the unidentified writer demands 50,000 dollars to reveal, with more exact details, the existence of Adolf Hitler in the savanna of Bogota. He furnished rather exact detail. Yesterday we received, place of origin unknown but definitely distant judging from the date, a letter from a man who claims to be a Colombian, and who disguises his name in order that he will not be identified. The unknown man claims that the story told by "Amigo, amigo, amigo" is the gospel truth, and he relates his sensational intervention in this "affair", connecting it with the assassination of Dr. Gaitán. The letter of "Mr. Eudoro Llama Seltz" follows:-

May 19, 1948.

Director of "El Tiempo".

Dear Sir:

There is nothing fantastic about the story which appeared in yesterday's edition of your newspaper which was signed with the pseudonym," Amigo, amigo, amigo", and gives an exact account of the presence of Hitler in the savanna of Bogota. Since January, 1945, approximately three years, I have been kept informed regarding the plans of the ex-Chancellor of Germany for the future. Purely through coincidence I became involved in these plans. They have been disclosed to me through a third person. In order to clarify the story, rather than confuse it, I want to tell you how I became a part of the gigantic plan against Soviet Communism.

Office Memorandum · UNITED STATES GOVERNMENT

TO : Director, FBI
DATE: July 14, 1948

: SAC, New York

SUBJECT: REPORTED PRESENCE OF ADOLPH HITLER
IN BOGOTA, COLOMBIA
SECURITY MATTER - G

On July 6, 1948, ▓▓▓▓▓▓▓▓▓▓▓▓▓▓▓▓▓▓▓ NYC, a Colombian by birth but now a naturalized United States citizen, came to the office with two newspaper clippings from the publication "El Tiempo", Bogota, Colombia. One of these clippings is from the issue of June 20, 1948, the other from the issue of June 24, 1948. She also presented a copy of the newspaper "Nueva York al Dia" of May 22, 1948, pointing particularly to the front page and page 5.

Photostatic copies of each clipping, and of the front page and page 5 of the newspaper mentioned, are being forwarded herewith as a matter of information. It will be noted they deal with a current story that ADOLPH HITLER is now in Bogota, Colombia.

It should also be noted that ▓▓▓▓▓▓▓▓ mentioned receiving a rumor in correspondence with friends in Colombia to the effect that a revolution is expected in that country on July 20 next, when the Liberals are expected to try to prevent the Conservatives from assembling the Congress.

Enclosures - 4

JMF/dht
100-0

Date: July 16, 1948

To: Director
Central Intelligence Agency
2430 E Street, N. W.
Washington, D. C.
Attention: ~~[redacted]~~

From: John Edgar Hoover, Director, Federal Bureau of Investigation

Subject: ADOLF HITLER;
MARTIN BORMANN
INTERNAL SECURITY - MISCELLANEOUS

RECORDED - 53

~~[redacted]~~ New York, New York, recently furnished this Bureau with a letter written in the German language, received by an employee of his office. This letter furnished information relative to the possible whereabouts of Adolf Hitler and Martin Bormann. ~~[redacted]~~ made the following comment with regard to this letter:

"The spelling within the letter as well as of the address shows that the writer is an uneducated man or a non-German. This also can be concluded from the fact that he wrote 'Stott Unita' behind New York which tends to show that the writer may be an Italian. There are two mistakes in the address; he wrote the word 'Redaktion' with a 'ck' instead of simple 'k' and ~~[redacted]~~ whose name appears on the envelope writes his name ~~[redacted]~~"

The following is an English translation of the German language letter mentioned above:

"Cavalesse (Trento Province), Italy,
At the end of May 1948.

"Dear Doctor:

"Last autumn an issue of the New Yorker Staats-Zeitung came into our possession. I believe that it was the issue of October 19.

"In it ~~[redacted]~~ the English author, Trevor-Roper, respectively his allegedly exact confirmation of the death of Adolf Hitler and Martin Bormann.

Letter to Director, Central Intelligence Agency

"The writer of this letter has no intention of contesting the historic confirmation of the named author in a frank manner or arguing about it in any way. But before the death of the two shall be considered final for all times to come, it may be worthwhile to examine the following:

"In the little community of Bobovo, Tonikva parish, District Šmarje pri Jelšah, Yugoslavia, two men have lived for three years. One of them rather tall, rather slender with a Kaiser-beard, that is a beard as worn by the late Emperor Franz Joseph, which was simply called Kaiser-bear in old Austria. Hair combed upwards.

"The other one is smaller, but stouter, with dark hair, mustache, both exactly like Hitler used to comb respectively cut it.

"Both men, known there as merchants returned from South America, live very modestly, but are very generous with the peasants and supposed to be extremely rich.

"They live with ▮▮▮▮▮▮▮▮▮▮ live very modest, receive no one without previous announcement and thorough examination, are strictly guarded by own guards. Mostly they rove about in the forests of the near Bacher Mountains. Also when they are at home, it is always said that they are travelling or on tours, etc. And there it is an unwritten law not to talk about the two; strangers are always told that nothing is known about them. The peasants and gendarmes of the surrounding localities have been bribed with large sums of money and bound by obligation to keep silent... In short, nobody knows them or anything about them.

"Nevertheless it would be advisable to look at the two by the use of an innocent trick, before Hitler's and Bormann's death is definitely accepted as a historic fact.

"Bobovo can be reached as follows: Coming from the north on the former Austrian southern railroad, from Marburg (Maribor) to the Poglawa railroad station. From there a walk on foot for half an hour, mostly through forest. Under any innocent pretext a guide can be secured by the station master to lead you to ▮▮▮▮▮▮
▮▮▮▮ both in Bobovo,

Letter to Director, Central Intelligence Agency

"From the south, Laibach (Ljubljana) Cilli (Celje) Prebolno. Next station is Konikwa. Leave the train, go about half an hour on foot, guide necessary. Or continue to the next station to Lipoglava. Then as above.

"Good luck! Skill necessary—keep your mouth shut.

"The men are known under the names: ▓▓▓▓▓ the taller one) and ▓▓▓▓▓ (the smaller one). His first name in the latter case is correct by accident. Lipoglav is the sixth station from Maribor in southerly direction.

"Please, never mention my name."

The reliability of the writer of the above letter is unknown and there is no record pertaining to him in the files of this Bureau. This information is being furnished to you for whatever action you deem appropriate under the circumstances.

It is requested that no dissemination of this material be made outside of your Department.

cc: Director of Intelligence
General Staff
Department of the Army
The Pentagon
Washington 25, D. C.
Attention: ▓▓▓▓▓ Chief
▓▓▓▓ Security Group

- 3 -

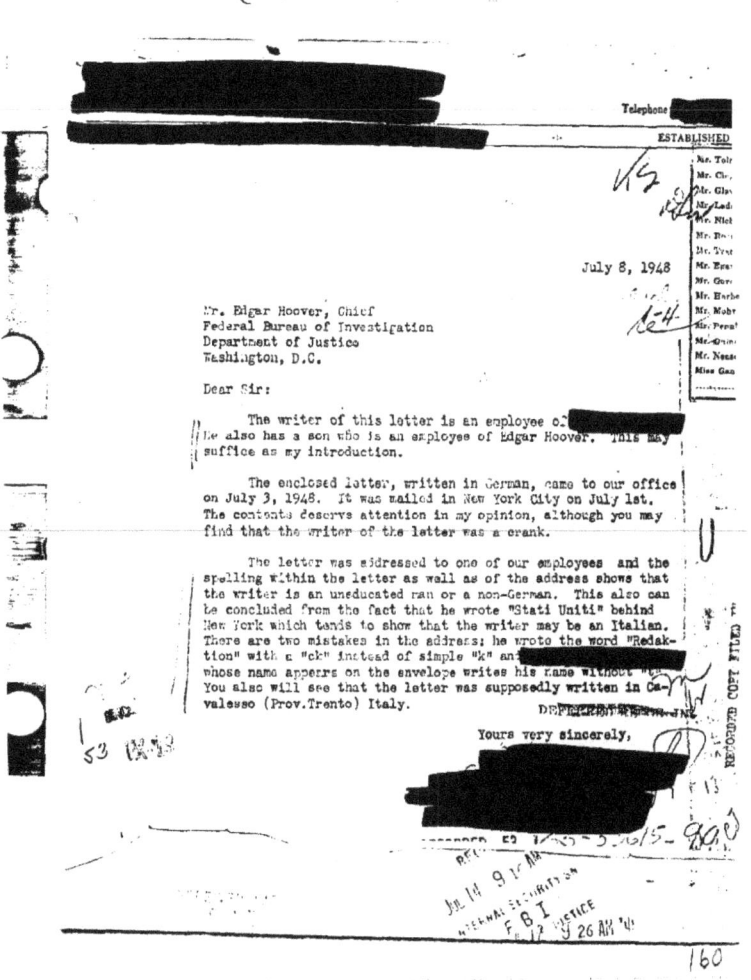

July 8, 1948

Mr. Edgar Hoover, Chief
Federal Bureau of Investigation
Department of Justice
Washington, D.C.

Dear Sir:

The writer of this letter is an employee of [redacted]. He also has a son who is an employee of Edgar Hoover. This may suffice as my introduction.

The enclosed letter, written in German, came to our office on July 3, 1948. It was mailed in New York City on July 1st. The contents deserve attention in my opinion, although you may find that the writer of the letter was a crank.

The letter was addressed to one of our employees and the spelling within the letter as well as of the address shows that the writer is an uneducated man or a non-German. This also can be concluded from the fact that he wrote "Stati Uniti" behind New York which tends to show that the writer may be an Italian. There are two mistakes in the address; he wrote the word "Redaktion" with a "ck" instead of simple "k" and [redacted] whose name appears on the envelope writes his name without [redacted]. You also will see that the letter was supposedly written in Cavalesso (Prov. Trento) Italy.

Yours very sincerely,

Office Memorandum • UNITED STATES GOVERNMENT

TO : H. B. Fletcher
FROM : L. N. Conroy
SUBJECT: ADOLF HITLER;
    Informant

DATE: October 10, 1948

███████████████████████████████ Washington, D. C. telephonically contacted the writer at 1:40 A.M. and advised she operates a rooming house at the above address. ███████ wished to report that she believes a guest who has been at her home for the past few weeks is Adolf Hitler, this belief being based solely on the fact that he looks somewhat like him. This person whose name is ███████ (full name unknown) resides there with his wife and grown son.

███████'s conversation was incoherent and she is obviously demented. She stated she contacted the Bureau not long ago at a time when she was being persecuted and was referred to the local police.

ACTION:

None. File.

LNC:BHW

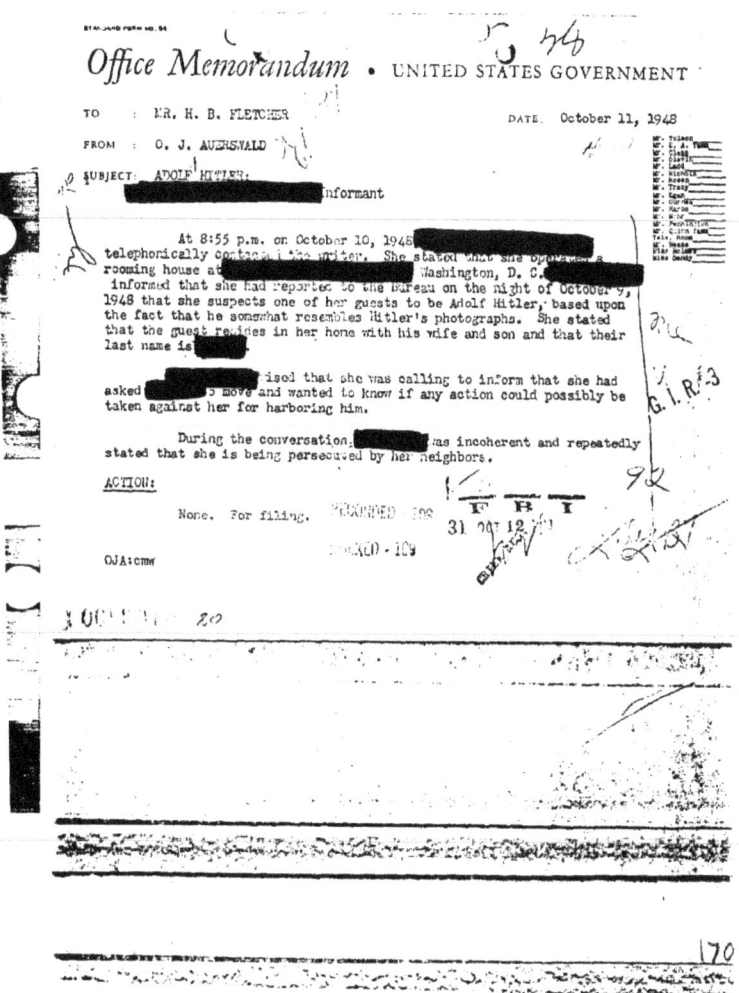

Office Memorandum • UNITED STATES GOVERNMENT

TO : MR. H. B. FLETCHER
FROM : O. J. AUERSWALD
DATE: October 11, 1948
SUBJECT: ADOLF HITLER
███████████ Informant

At 8:55 p.m. on October 10, 1948, ██████ telephonically contacted the writer. She stated that she operates a rooming house at ██████████████ Washington, D.C. ██████ informed that she had reported to the Bureau on the night of October 9, 1948 that she suspects one of her guests to be Adolf Hitler, based upon the fact that he somewhat resembles Hitler's photographs. She stated that the guest resides in her home with his wife and son and that their last name is ███████.

████████ advised that she was calling to inform that she had asked ████████ to move and wanted to know if any action could possibly be taken against her for harboring him.

During the conversation, ████████ was incoherent and repeatedly stated that she is being persecuted by her neighbors.

ACTION:

None. For filing.

OJA:cmw

Sir the reason that I am writing for information is, that I have been watc- a man there in St. Louis for over a year. He has all of Hitlers actions such as his habit of sliding his hands into his trousers, he is an expertly trained goose stepper with hitler's swagger. if you co- see him, as I have seen him with a dog p— at his leash, and this fellow following, wit— his hat down over his eyes, and his goose steps in full swing, you would be tempted to say that there goes Adolph Hitler. ▮▮▮▮▮▮ was sick, he was a doing a lot of hammering at night, and I had the police after him. he was up on a balcony, and I had him moved, he said to me. go ahead, and have me arrested, it wont hurt me. I have been in jail before, I have no fear of your jail

You would have said he was Hitler then by the way he thrust his chin out, and the tone of voice he used.

This man to my estimation is foreign born, and I am sure no american born man could ever have developed the goose step such as this man had.

I always did say, and still say that Hitler had left Germany at least 1½ y before the fall of Berlin.

If this fellow is not Hitler, he is an exact duplicate.

The picture of Hitler reviewing his troops just a few months before the fall of Berlin was not Adolph Hitler. I also say Hitler is not dead.

Office Memorandum · UNITED STATES GOVERNMENT

TO : DIRECTOR, FBI DATE: March 18, 1949
FROM : SAC, ST. LOUIS
SUBJECT: ▓▓▓▓▓▓▓▓▓▓▓▓ - Informant
INFORMATION CONCERNING

Reference is made to bulet dated 12-15-48, addressed to ▓▓▓▓ ▓▓▓▓▓▓▓▓▓▓▓▓▓▓▓▓▓▓▓▓▓▓▓▓▓. Louis, Mo. to which an addendum was attached directing this office to interview ▓▓▓▓▓▓▓ concerning his report that he believed ADOLPH HITLER was in St. Louis. In accordance with Bureau instructions, ▓▓▓▓▓▓ was immediately contacted by telephone and an interview requested. Due to the nature of ▓▓▓▓▓▓ employment, it was not possible to interview him at his home until January 11, 1949. At that time, ▓▓▓▓▓ advised that he has known a man, named ▓▓▓▓▓▓ for about two years and that ▓▓▓▓▓ has taken over the management or ownership of the building where ▓▓▓▓▓ resides, and has been attempting to evict ▓▓▓▓ from his living quarters on the second floor. ▓▓▓▓▓ has developed an intense dislike for ▓▓▓ and presently sends his monthly rent check to ▓▓▓▓ by registered mail, return receipt requested, although ▓▓▓▓ resides immediately below RAMEY.

According to ▓▓▓▓▓▓▓▓▓▓ operates ▓▓▓▓▓▓▓▓▓▓▓ Ave. and also operates another place of business someplace on South Broadway, St. Louis. ▓▓▓ has no other reason for thinking that ▓▓▓▓ is ADOLPH HITLER except that ▓▓▓ is German, speaks with a definite German accent and refused to tell his life's history.

Preliminary inquiry made to determine who ▓▓▓▓▓ is has resulted in very little information of value. Local credit bureaus have no information on him, and St. Louis Police files contain only records of minor arrests for peace disturbance, etc. A check ▓▓▓▓▓▓▓▓▓▓▓▓▓▓▓▓▓▓▓▓▓▓▓▓▓▓▓▓ noted in front of ▓▓▓▓▓▓▓▓▓▓▓▓▓ disclosed it was issued ▓▓▓▓▓▓▓▓▓▓▓ in the area of St. Louis Co., Mo. ▓▓▓▓▓▓ confectionery business, advised that ▓▓▓▓ speaks with a definite German accent, and is described as about sixty-three years of age, five ft. seven inches, one-hundred and seventy lbs., stocky build, grey hair, partly bald, wears glasses. The files of the St. Louis office contained no information concerning ▓▓▓▓▓.

▓▓▓▓▓▓▓▓▓▓▓▓▓▓▓▓▓▓▓▓▓▓ reliable German Informant, advised that he has never heard of ▓▓▓▓ but has volunteered to become acquainted with ▓▓▓ by making purchases at ▓▓▓ place of business. Informant speaks fluent German and will be able to gain the confidence of KRAUSE because of their mutual interest in Germany. No active investigation is being made in this matter since it is apparent that ▓▓▓ reported ▓▓▓ chiefly because of his intense dislike for ▓▓▓ and not because of any real evidence indicating that ▓▓▓ is actually ADOLPH HITLER. If ▓▓▓ reports any information of value, the Bureau will be advised; otherwise, the case will be closed by this office.

H.H.X. declares that he went to Colombia in 1944 with the help of some Brazilians, after fleeing from Himmler's agents who followed him wherever he went.

On February 1 (?), 1945, he was visited by a German who claimed to know him well and be very familiar with his record as a Nazi spy in America. He showed him documents to prove this, and then showed him an order which stated that H.H.X. was to collaborate with this German in finding the best way to help Hitler and his followers to enter Colombia secretly and stealthily. On pain of slow torture and death, H.H.X. was forced to aid in this plan. In accordance with definite orders received, he got in touch with Agent Z, contact man no. 16, at the end of February, 1945. Agent Z. traced for him on a Colombian map, possible points from where Hitler, Martin Bormann, and other Germans could enter secretly. He referred me to Colombian Agent X, contact man no. 5-Col, with whom he had already discussed and approved plan "Zert" re secret immigration of Hitler and the others, based on cardinal point "W-Z-ph", which coincides exactly with the most extremely southwestern point of Colombian territory.

Shortly after this, H.H.X. became ill and was in a hospital in Bogota for some length of time. He remained in the hospital until after the German Legation had been seized by democratic forces.

H.H.X. asserts that he is ready to prove that the story told by Isidoro Llana Salta is true. He will give all the information he has, including the names of various Colombians who participated in the "affair", providing his own name and identity remain secret. He wishes that the interview will be secret and confidential, because of the fear that he will be assassinated by other agents, if any publicity is given him. In return for his providing these proofs of Hitler's plan to enter Colombia, etc. he wishes to be compensated financially in order that he may return to his family in Germany, in the United States Zone of Occupation. He claims to be still persecuted by Nazi agents.

Summarized by:
Rose R. Offenbacher
July 27, 1948.

2. Condition

The folds, tears, creases, and stains were examined for indications of simulation, but none was found, the condition throughout being that of papers folded together which have been maintained in that position for some time during which they were subjected to moisture and wear.

The visible transfer from one sheet to another of stains from the typewriting and ink were studied from the standpoint that they might be the result of mechanical reproduction (using the jelly Hectograph method) or be the result of simulation. Even where no appreciable transfer from one paper to another has taken place, the ink lines and typing have run into the surrounding paper. This, however, is usually of a different shade of color from the original ink, in some parts being a radically different color. This occurs normally, because some inks are composed of dyes of more than one color which combine to create the ink "color" but dissolve and run in different degrees of solution. Thus "blue" ink may run "green" (as in this case).

The fact that these natural (but unnatural appearing) phenomena occur on these papers is evidence of genuineness since persons preparing forgeries usually take care to match the color closely. The fading produced by different concentrations of dye in water is also very difficult to simulate without leaving evidence. No such evidence was found.

The transfers of writings (typewriting as well as ink) show that the papers were out of place in sequence and disarranged in position when the dampening occurred. This is typically accidental, not planned.

3. Typewriting

The Marriage paper, C1 and C2, was typed on a machine equipped with type designs matching those of known German manufacture, "Hauman Erika", and with German alphabet characters.

The other two documents were written on a different typewriter, the space adjustments of which remained set for both papers, Q3 through Q5 and Q6 through Q17. This is a Medium Roman design of type with "uncial" or "Gothic" numerals. No exact match of this design appears in the FBI file of standards, which is without a few European designs since the war. As Medium Roman design is used in the known specimens K1 through K14, a close comparison was made. It was found that K13, signed Bormann on the letterhead of the NSDAP 4 April 1945, was a very close match for the two wills, Q3 to Q17 inclusive. No conclusion could be reached whether they were written on this identical typewriter as the moistening of Q3 to Q17 inclusive has somewhat obscured the microscopic appearance of the impressions and mechanical defects suitable for positive identification are not prominent.

If there were a purpose in this, it might be possible to definitely identify the typewriter used on Q3 to Q17 inclusive if known specimens could be

Continued next page

Epilogue

It is claimed that Hitler was suffering the symptoms of Parkinson's disease and could have only lived a few more years with the medicine available in the 1940s. It is unclear from the theory when he died.

Following the declassification of FBI documents exploring whether Hitler might have escaped his apparent fate in Berlin, where he is widely believed to have died in 1945, *Hunting Hitler* -a History Channel television show was conceived and it ran for three seasons between 2015 and 2018, followed by a two-hour special in 2020.

The *Führerbunker* was an air-raid shelter located near the Reich Chancellery in Berlin, Germany. It was part of a subterranean bunker complex constructed in two phases in 1936 and 1944. It was the last of the Führer Headquarters used by Adolf Hitler during World War II.

The series explores how might Hitler have escaped from the *Führerbunker* in Berlin at the end of World War II, where might he have gone, and whether he plotted a Fourth Reich.

The show was hosted in Los Angeles by CIA veteran Bob Baer and war crimes investigator John Cencich. Utilizing a database of intelligence files from the FBI, CIA, MI6, and other international authorities, they look for information regarding the survival of Adolf Hitler or any of his right-hand men.

His team discovered Hitler could have been planning to escape from his bunker to Tempelhof airport by using a massive network of tunnels under the Berlin city.

EPILOGUE

[1] Source: HISTORY channel series *Hunting Hitler*

The television series shows Nazi Interrogation Archiv Datenbank (NIAD) has a database of interviews of Hitler's inner circles, conducted at the Nuremberg trials (a series of military tribunals held following World War II by the Allied forces for the prosecution of prominent leaders of Nazi Germany) where Nazi Admiral Karl von Puttkamer -Hitler's naval adjutant, Office of the Wehrmacht says: We left Berlin by air in the early morning of 21 of April. It was still dark when we left about three in the morning. I left from Berlin-Staaken; others left from Tempelhof. We were about eight or ten aircraft. ...The first plane was loaded with Hitler's personal property.

"Tempelhof airport was in under Allied control in those seven days after the flight mentioned in the testimony."

Tempelhof, a locality of Berlin, is the location of the former Tempelhof Airport, one of the earliest commercial airports in the world.

EPILOGUE

[2] Source: HISTORY channel series *Hunting Hitler*

Did Hitler Escape His Bunker Using A Subway Tunnel? | Hunting Hitler

[3] Source: HISTORY channel series *Hunting Hitler*

EPILOGUE

The former airport and surroundings are now a park called Tempelhofer Feld, making it the largest inner-city open space in the world.

Concealing his identity, a person was interviewed who was part of Hitler's youth Army. He remembers distinctly, one night, he was told by his bosses, don't shoot any flight overhead tonight because there could be German aeroplanes.

Did Hitler Escape His Bunker Using A Subway Tunnel? | Hunting Hitler

[4] Source: HISTORY channel series *Hunting Hitler*

The team investigated a massive network of nazi tunnels under the city, constructed during the war and accessible from Hitler's bunker. They traced out a link between tunnels and six sub-ways towards Tempelhof airport.

Interestingly, 'Bhagwanji' narrates about the secret of Bose's escape with minute details as noted by *Charanik*: He said to the adjutant, remember my instructions, I could not tell you the details.

... Then the Mahānāyaka boarded and departed for an unknown destination" (loosely translated from *Oi Mahamanab Ase*, Akhaṇḍa sanskaraṇa, 2010, 87-88).

EPILOGUE

'Bhagwanji' further narrates: He planned his disappearance, Jewelry and Treasure were packed for dropping at a place of his disappearance.

First Bomber was a dummy flight with the publicity of Him, Kimura, and others.

Real Bomber left after, for unknown destination (*Oi Mahamanab Ase*, Akhaṇḍa sanskaraṇa, 2010, 308).

There is a strange similarity in the possible escape plan of Netaji Subhas Chandra Bose and Adolf Hitler, first by plane and then by submarine to an undisclosed destination.

In Season 3 of the *Hunting Hitler* series (2017–2018), Bob Baer -the former CIA Operative recruits prominent terrorist targeting officer Nada Bakos. Enacting the hunting strategy which led to the capture of Osama bin Laden, the team finds two planned escape routes for Hitler out of Germany. To the south, Tim Kennedy -U.S. Army Special Forces operator and former MMA fighter, and James Holland -WWII historian, discover a tunnel system under Hitler's home. To the north, Lenny DePaul -former U.S. Marshals commander and Gerrard Williams -investigative journalist and historian, investigates a hidden Nazi compound.

DePaul and Williams make a startling discovery in a sabotaged aircraft hangar in northern Germany. Mike Simpson -a medical doctor, airborne ranger, and special forces operator and Holland scan an Austrian lake in search of a large cache of secret Nazi documents.

In Norway, Kennedy and Williams explore a hydroelectric plant where the Nazis were dangerously close to producing a nuclear weapon. Simpson and Holland investigate a cabin high in the Austrian Alps where Hitler's top associate made the ultimate sacrifice.

At the bottom of an Arctic fjord in Norway, Kennedy dives on Nazi relics that may blow the case wide open. Simpson and Holland encounter a smuggler who leads them to Nazi castle on the Italian border.

EPILOGUE

Simpson and Holland excavate the grounds of a remote Alpine hotel in search of buried Nazi dead drops. In Rome, DePaul and Williams make a shocking discovery that implicates some of the world's most powerful people.

At a lagoon in Uruguay, Kennedy and Simpson uncover evidence of a long-range seaplane that was shuttling Nazis all around the continent. In Buenos Aires, Kennedy and Williams convince an informant to share a massive cache of explosive documents that could unravel the clandestine global Nazi network known as *Die Spinne*.

On the trail of Josef Mengele, Kennedy and Simpson investigate a key Nazi support point in Uruguay: Rincón del Bonete dam. Simpson and DePaul review newly declassified Chilean files that reveal a secret plot to attack the United States.

Kennedy and Williams discover a mysterious militarized Nazi compound in the jungle of Paraguay. Simpson and DePaul explore an alleged Nazi concentration camp in Chile before an anonymous source leads them to a microfilm copy of Hitler's last will and testament. Baer presents the compiled evidence of Hitler's possible escape.

But, in 2020, the *Hunting Hitler* team member James Holland wrote on Twitter, "I was certainly interested in learning more about how Nazis escaped, but was *very* careful never to mention on film that I thought either Hitler or Bormann escaped. Because they didn't.

He has reportedly described the series as "absolute nonsense" on his podcast *We Have Ways of Making You Talk* in 2021.

Secret CIA files reveal, Hitler openly admitted fantasising about himself as Jesus Christ. Then comes this revealing theory. After Hitler breathed his last in Kashmir, his body was taken to a tomb in "Rozabal", reputed to be the final resting place of Christ -the least likely place anyone would expect, the fugitive Führer could there be buried.

But because the site is holy, an exhumation is unlikely any time soon because of strict laws safeguarding spiritual sites.

EPILOGUE

Yet while the theory remains that Hitler escaped his bunker in Berlin and fled to a safe haven, Russia insists he did die, and it has the bones to prove it.

According to Russian government authorities, the Führer's skull and jaw with some teeth intact and is safely stored away in one of Vladimir Putin's vaults in Moscow.

This has raised the prospect of Hitler being cloned should any DNA remain in his bones. But the remains have not been confirmed as Adolf's and some claim the Soviet Union faked the discovery to avoid the embarrassment of Hitler escaping under their noses. Yet until the bones with the Russians and those in Kashmir can be subject to DNA tests, we will never know the true fate of Adolf Hitler.

CPSIA information can be obtained
at www.ICGtesting.com
Printed in the USA
LVHW100813300523
748338LV00003B/36